CONSTITUTIO
ADMINISTRA

Second edition

Richard Clements

Series editors: Amy Sixsmith and David Sixsmith

First published in 2021 by Fink Publishing Ltd
Second edition published in 2023

British Library Cataloguing in Publication Data
A catalogue record for this book is available from the British Library
ISBN: 9781914213595

This book is also available in various ebook formats.
Ebook ISBN: 9781914213601

Multiple-choice questions advisor: Mark Thomas
Cover and text design by BMLD (bmld.uk)
Production and typesetting by Westchester Publishing Services (UK)
Commissioning by R Taylor Publishing Services
Development editing by Peter Hooper
Editorial management by Llinos Edwards
Indexing by Terence Halliday

Fink Publishing Ltd
E-mail: hello@revise4law.co.uk
www.revise4law.co.uk

Contents

This book incorporates the updates to the SQE Assessment Specification published in April 2023 which came into force from 1 September 2023. Please note that, unless otherwise expressly stated, the law covered in this book applies in both England and Wales.

Contributors

THE AUTHOR

Richard Clements has taught constitutional law at a number of universities including the University of the West of England and Exeter University. His teaching has incorporated many professional law courses and for many years he has used multiple-choice questions as a method of assessment. He is the author of *Complete Equity and Trusts* and *Questions and Answers on Constitutional and Administrative Law*.

SERIES EDITORS

Amy Sixsmith is a senior lecturer in law and programme leader for LLB at the University of Sunderland, and a senior fellow of the Higher Education Academy.

David Sixsmith is assistant professor at Northumbria Law School and a senior fellow of the Higher Education Academy.

Introduction to Revise SQE

Welcome to *Revise SQE*, a new series of revision guides designed to help you in your preparation for, and achievement in, the Solicitors Qualifying Examination 1 (SQE1) assessment. SQE1 is designed to assess what the Solicitors Regulation Authority (SRA) refers to as 'functioning legal knowledge' (FLK); this is the legal knowledge and competencies required of a newly qualified solicitor in England and Wales. The SRA has chosen single best answer multiple-choice questions (MCQs) to test this knowledge, and *Revise SQE* is here to help.

PREPARING YOURSELF FOR SQE

The SQE is the new route to qualification for aspiring solicitors, introduced in September 2021 as one of the final stages towards qualification as a solicitor. The SQE consists of two parts:

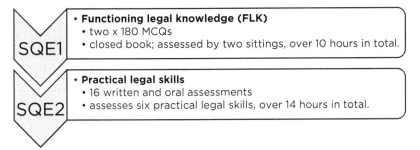

SQE1
- **Functioning legal knowledge (FLK)**
  - two x 180 MCQs
  - closed book; assessed by two sittings, over 10 hours in total.

SQE2
- **Practical legal skills**
  - 16 written and oral assessments
  - assesses six practical legal skills, over 14 hours in total.

In addition to the above, any candidate will have to undertake two years' qualifying work experience. More information on the SQE assessments can be found on the SRA website; this revision guide series will focus on FLK and preparation for SQE1.

It is important to note that the SQE can be perceived to be a 'harder' set of assessments than the Legal Practice Course (LPC). The reason for this, explained by the SRA, is that the LPC is designed to prepare candidates for 'day one' of their training contract; the SQE, on the other hand, is designed to prepare candidates for 'day one' of being a newly qualified solicitor. Indeed, the SRA has chosen the SQE1 assessment to be 'closed book' (ie without permitting use of any materials) on the basis that a newly qualified solicitor would know all of the information being tested, without having to refer to books or other sources.

With that in mind, and a different style of assessments in place, it is understandable that many readers may feel nervous or wary of the SQE. This is especially so given that this style of assessment is likely to be different from what readers will have experienced before. In this *Introduction* and revision guide series, we hope to alleviate some of those concerns with guidance on preparing for the SQE assessment, tips on how to approach single best answer MCQs and expertly written guides to aid in your revision.

What does SQE1 entail?

SQE1 consists of two assessments, containing 180 single best answer MCQs each (360 MCQs in total). The table below breaks down what is featured in each of these assessments.

Assessment	Contents of assessment ('functioning legal knowledge')
FLK assessment 1	• Business law and practice • Dispute resolution • Contract • Tort • The legal system (the legal system of England and Wales and sources of law, constitutional and administrative law and European Union law and legal services)
FLK assessment 2	• Property practice • Wills and the administration of estates • Solicitors accounts • Land law • Trusts • Criminal law and practice

Please be aware that in addition to the above, ethics and professional conduct will be examined pervasively across the two assessments (ie it could crop up anywhere).

Each substantive topic is allocated a percentage of the assessment paper (eg 'legal services' will form 12–16% of the FLK1 assessment) and is broken down further into 'core principles'. Candidates are advised to read the SQE1 Assessment Specification in full (available on the SRA website). We have also provided a *Revise SQE checklist* to help you in your preparation and revision for SQE1 (see below).

HOW DO I PREPARE FOR SQE1?

Given the vastly different nature of SQE1 compared to anything you may have done previously, it can be quite daunting to consider how you could possibly prepare for 360 single best answer MCQs, spanning 11 different substantive topics (especially given that it is 'closed book'). The *Revise SQE FAQs* below, however, will set you off on the right path to success.

Revise SQE FAQs

Question	Answer
1. Where do I start?	We would advise that you begin by reviewing the assessment specification for SQE1. You need to identify what subject matter can be assessed under each substantive topic. For each topic, you should honestly ask yourself whether you would be prepared to answer an MCQ on that topic in SQE1.
	We have helped you in this process by providing a *Revise SQE checklist* on our website (revise4law.co.uk) that allows you to read the subject matter of each topic and identify where you consider your knowledge to be at any given time. We have also helpfully cross-referenced each topic to a chapter and page of our *Revise SQE* revision guides.
2. Do I need to know legal authorities, such as case law?	In the majority of circumstances, candidates are not required to know or use legal authorities. This includes statutory provisions, case law or procedural rules. Of course, candidates will need to be aware of legal principles deriving from common law and statute.
	There may be occasions, however, where the assessment specification does identify a legal authority (such as *Rylands v Fletcher* in tort law). In this case, candidates will be required to know the name of that case, the principles of that case and how to apply that case to the facts of an MCQ. These circumstances are clearly highlighted in the assessment specification and candidates are advised to ensure they engage with those legal authorities in full.

Revise SQE FAQs (continued)

Question	Answer
3. Do I need to know the history behind a certain area of law?	While understanding the history and development of a certain area of law is beneficial, there is no requirement for you to know or prepare for any questions relating to the development of the law (eg in criminal law, candidates will not need to be aware of the development from objective to subjective recklessness). SQE1 will be testing a candidate's knowledge of the law as stated at the date of the assessment.
4. Do I need to be aware of academic opinion or proposed reforms to the law?	Candidates preparing for SQE1 do not need to focus on critical evaluation of the law, or proposed reforms to the law either.
5. How do I prepare for single best answer MCQs?	See our separate *Revise SQE* guide on preparing for single best answer MCQs below.

Where does *Revise SQE* come into it?

The *Revise SQE* series of revision guides is designed to aid your revision and consolidate your understanding; the series is not designed to replace your substantive learning of the SQE1 topics. We hope that this series will provide clarity as to assessment focus, useful tips for sitting SQE1 and act as a general revision aid.

There are also materials on our website to help you prepare and revise for the SQE1, such as a *Revise SQE checklist*. This *checklist* is designed to help you identify which substantive topics you feel confident about heading into the exam – see below for an example.

Revise SQE checklist

Constitutional and Administrative Law

SQE content	Corresponding chapter	*Revise SQE checklist*		
Judicial review • Application for judicial review	Chapter 7, pages 118–122	I do not know this subject and I am not ready for SQE1 ☐	I partially know this subject, but I am not ready for SQE1 ☐	I know this subject and I am ready for SQE1 ☐

Constitutional and Administrative Law (continued)

SQE content	Corresponding chapter	Revise SQE checklist		
Judicial review • The grounds for judicial review	Chapter 7, pages 122–123	I do not know this subject and I am not ready for SQE1 ☐	I partially know this subject, but I am not ready for SQE1 ☐	I know this subject and I am ready for SQE1 ☐
Judicial review • Irrationality	Chapter 7, pages 124–127	I do not know this subject and I am not ready for SQE1 ☐	I partially know this subject, but I am not ready for SQE1 ☐	I know this subject and I am ready for SQE1 ☐

PREPARING FOR SINGLE BEST ANSWER MCQS

As discussed above, SQE1 will be a challenging assessment for all candidates. This is partly due to the quantity of information a candidate must be aware of in two separate sittings. In addition, however, an extra complexity is added due to the nature of the assessment itself: MCQs.

The SRA has identified that MCQs are the most appropriate way to test a candidate's knowledge and understanding of fundamental legal principles. While this may be the case, it is likely that many candidates have little, if any, experience of MCQs as part of their previous study. Even if a candidate does have experience of MCQs, SQE1 will feature a special form of MCQs known as 'single best answer' questions.

What are single best answer MCQs and what do they look like?

Single best answer MCQs are a specialised form of question, used extensively in other fields such as in training medical professionals. The idea behind single best answer MCQs is that the multitude of options available to a candidate may each bear merit, sharing commonalities and correct statements of law or principle, but only one option is absolutely correct (in the sense that it is the 'best' answer). In this regard, single best answer MCQs are different from traditional MCQs. A traditional MCQ will feature answers that are implausible in the sense that the distractors are 'obviously wrong'. Indeed, distractors in a traditional MCQ are often very dissimilar, resulting in a candidate being able to spot answers that are clearly wrong with greater ease.

In a well-constructed single best answer MCQ, on the other hand, each option should look equally attractive given their similarities and subtle differences. The skill of the candidate will be identifying which, out of the options provided, is the single best answer. This requires a much greater level of engagement with the question than a traditional MCQ would require; candidates must take the time to read the questions carefully in the exam.

For SQE1, single best answer MCQs will be structured as follows:

A woman is charged with battery, having thrown a rock towards another person intending to scare them. The rock hits the person in the head, causing no injury. The woman claims that she never intended that the rock hit the person, but the prosecution allege that the woman was reckless as to whether the rock would hit the other person.

The factual scenario. First, the candidate will be provided with a factual scenario that sets the scene for the question to be asked.

Which of the following is the most accurate statement regarding the test for recklessness in relation to a battery?

The question. Next, the candidate will be provided with the question (known as the 'stem') that they must find the single best answer to.

A. There must have been a risk that force would be applied by the rock, and that the reasonable person would have foreseen that risk and unjustifiably taken it.
B. There must have been a risk that force would be applied by the rock, and that the woman should have foreseen that risk and unjustifiably taken it.
C. There must have been a risk that force would be applied by the rock, and that the woman must have foreseen that risk and unjustifiably taken it.
D. There must have been a risk that force would be applied by the rock, and that both the woman and the reasonable person should have foreseen that risk and unjustifiably taken it.
E. There must have been a risk that force would be applied by the rock, but there is no requirement that the risk be foreseen.

The possible answers. Finally, the candidate will be provided with **five** possible answers. There is only one single best answer that must be chosen. The other answers, known as 'distractors', are not the 'best' answer available.

Now that you know what the MCQs will look like on SQE1, let us talk about how you may go about tackling an MCQ.

How do I tackle single best answer MCQs?

No exact art exists in terms of answering single best answer MCQs; your success depends on your subject knowledge and understanding of how that subject knowledge can be applied. Despite this, there are tips and tricks that may be helpful for you to consider when confronted with a single best answer MCQ.

1. Read the question twice	2. Understand the question being asked	3. Select the answer if you know it outright	4. If not, employ a process of elimination	5. Take an educated and reasoned guess	6. Skip and come back to it later

1. Read the entire question at least twice

This sounds obvious but is so often overlooked. You are advised to read the entire question once, taking in all relevant pieces of information, understanding what the question is asking you and being aware of the options available. Once you have done that, read the entire question again and this time pay careful attention to the wording that is used.

- **In the factual scenario:** Does it use any words that stand out? Do any words used have legal bearing? What are you told, and what are you not told?
- **In the stem:** What are you being asked? Are there certain words to look out for (eg 'should', 'must', 'will', 'shall')?
- **In the answers:** What are the differences between each option? Are they substantial differences or subtle differences? Do any differences turn on a word or a phrase?

You should be prepared to give each question at least two viewings to mitigate any misunderstandings or oversights.

2. Understand the question being asked

It is important first that you understand what the question is asking of you. The SRA has identified that the FLK assessments may consist of single best answer MCQs that, for example,

- require the candidate to simply identify a correct legal principle or rule
- require the candidate to not only identify the correct legal principle or rule, but also apply that principle or rule to the factual scenario
- provide the candidate with the correct legal principle or rule, but require the candidate to identify how it should be properly applied and/or the outcome of that proper application.

By first identifying what the question is seeking you to do, you can then understand what the creators of that question are seeking to test and how to approach the answers available.

3. Select the answer if you know it outright

You may feel as though a particular answer 'jumps out' at you, and that you are certain it is correct. It is very likely that the answer is correct. While you should be confident in your answers, do not allow your confidence (and perhaps overconfidence) to rush you into making a decision. Review all of your options one final time before you move on to the next question.

4. If you do not know the answer outright, employ a process of elimination

There may be situations in which the answer is not obvious from the outset. This may be due to the close similarities between different answers. Remember, it is the 'single best answer' that you are looking for. If you keep this in your mind, it will thereafter be easier to employ a process of elimination. Identify which answers you are sure are not correct (or not the 'best') and whittle down your options. Once you have only two options remaining, carefully scrutinise the wording used in both answers and look back to the question being asked. Identify what you consider to the be the best answer, in light of that question. Review your answer and move on to the next question.

5. Take an educated and reasoned guess

There may be circumstances, quite commonly, in which you do not know the answer to the question. In this circumstance, you should try as hard as possible to eliminate any distractors that you are positive are incorrect and then take an educated and reasoned guess based on the options available.

6. Skip and come back to it later

If time permits, you may think it appropriate to skip a question that you are unsure of and return to it before the end of the assessment. If you do so, we would advise

- that you make a note of what question you have skipped (for ease of navigation later on) and
- ensure you leave sufficient time for you to go back to that question before the end of the assessment.

The same advice is applicable to any question that you have answered but for which you remain unsure.

We hope that this brief guide will assist you in your preparation towards, and engagement with, single best answer MCQs.

GUIDED TOUR

Each chapter contains a number of features to help you revise, apply and test your knowledge.

Make sure you know   Each chapter begins with an overview of the main topics covered and why you need to understand them for the purpose of the SQE1 assessments.

SQE assessment advice   This identifies what you need to pay particular attention to in your revision as you work through the chapter.

What do you know already?   These questions help you to assess which topics you feel confident with and which topics you may need to spend more time on (and where to find them in the chapter).

Key term   Key terms are highlighted in bold where they first appear and defined in a separate box.

Exam warning   This feature offers advice on where it is possible to go wrong in the assessments.

Revision tip   Throughout the chapters are ideas to help you revise effectively and be best prepared for the assessment.

Summary   This handy box brings together key information in an easy to revise and remember form.

Practice example   These examples take a similar format to SQE-type questions and provide an opportunity to see how content might be applied to a scenario.

Procedural link   Where relevant, this element shows how a concept might apply to another procedural topic in the series.

Key point checklist   At the end of each chapter there is a bullet-point summary of its most important content.

Key terms and concepts   These are listed at the end of each chapter to help ensure you know, or can revise, terms and concepts you will need to be familiar with for the assessments.

SQE-style questions Five SQE-style questions on the chapter topic give you an opportunity to test your knowledge.

Answers to questions Check how you did with answers to both the quick knowledge test from the start of the chapter and the SQE questions at the end of the chapter.

Key cases, rules, statutes and instruments These list the key sources candidates need to be familiar with for the SQE assessment.

SQE1 TABLE OF LEGAL AUTHORITIES

The SQE1 Assessment Specification states the following in respect of legal authorities and their relevance to SQE1:

> On occasion in legal practice a case name or statutory provision, for example, is the term normally used to describe a legal principle or an area of law, or a rule or procedural step (eg *Rylands v Fletcher*, CPR Part 36, Section 25 notice). In such circumstances, candidates are required to know and be able to use such case names, statutory provisions etc. In all other circumstances candidates are not required to recall specific case names, or cite statutory or regulatory authorities.

This *SQE1 table of legal authorities* identifies the legal authorities you are required to know for the purpose of the SQE1 Functioning Legal Knowledge assessments for *Constitutional and Administrative Law.*

Legal authority	Corresponding *Revise SQE* chapter/pages
The Human Rights Act 1998	Chapter 1: The constitution and conventions, page 8
The Human Rights Act 1998	Chapter 2: Parliament, parliamentary sovereignty and parliamentary privilege, page 30
s 3	page 30
The Human Rights Act 1998	Chapter 3: Central government and devolved institutions, pages 50, 51, 52 and 54

(continued)

Legal authority	Corresponding *Revise SQE* chapter/pages
The Human Rights Act 1998	Chapter 5: Legislation, primary and secondary, page 88
s 10	page 88
The Human Rights Act 1998	Chapter 6: Public order law, pages 96 and 101
The Human Rights Act 1998	Chapter 8: Human rights, page 134
s 2	page 137
s 3	page 138
s 4	page 139
s 6	page 140
s 7	page 141
s 8	page 138
s 10	page 134
Schedule 1 Convention Rights	page 142

TABLE OF CASES

TABLE OF STATUTES

The constitution and conventions

■ MAKE SURE YOU KNOW

This chapter will explain what a constitution is, the difference between written and unwritten constitutions, the role of constitutional conventions and constitutional theories such as the separation of powers and the rule of law. You will need to know about these topics and be able to apply them to scenarios, problems and situations for your SQE1 assessment.

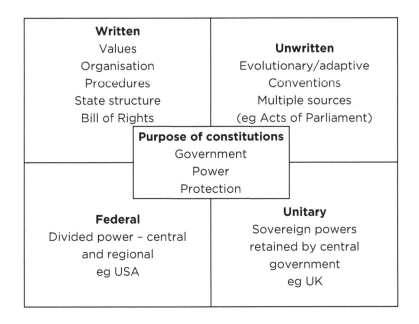

■ SQE ASSESSMENT ADVICE

The SQE1 Assessment Specification for constitutional and administrative law covers a wide range of topics, which might seem unconnected. To do well in the SQE1 assessment, it is essential that you understand how these topics fit together and this chapter aims to explain this.

As you work through this chapter, remember to pay particular attention in your revision to the following:
- The UK does not have a written constitution, which is unusual. That does not mean that it does not have a constitution.
- The UK has a constitution that applies to the whole country, but Scotland, Wales and Northern Ireland also have their own, different constitutional arrangements.
- The UK constitution is not just law, but also constitutional convention. Clearly identify what is a law and what is a convention.

■ WHAT DO YOU KNOW ALREADY?

Have a go at these questions before reading this chapter. If you find some difficult or cannot remember the answers, make a note to look more closely at that subtopic during your revision.

1) Why do countries have a constitution?
   [The purpose of a constitution, page 3]
2) A written constitution is one contained in an Act of Parliament. True or false?
   [Written and unwritten constitutions, page 3]
3) Why does the UK not have a written constitution?
   [The UK has an unwritten constitution, page 4]
4) What is the difference between a federal and a unitary state?
   [Federal or unitary constitutions, page 6]
5) Is any of the UK constitution legally enforceable?
   [The sources of the constitution, page 7]
6) Which of the following is correct? The royal prerogative:
   a) allows the King to govern the country
   b) allows the government to govern in the King's name
   c) gives the royal family immunity from the law.
   [The royal prerogative, page 9]
7) What are constitutional conventions?
   a) meetings of Parliament
   b) non-legal rules of the constitution
   c) international treaties.
   [Conventions, page 13]

CONSTITUTIONS

First, we need to define what a **constitution** is. This section will help you revise:

- the purpose of a constitution
- written and unwritten constitutions
- the contents of a constitution
- the UK's unwritten constitution
- federal or unitary constitutions.

The purpose of a constitution

Every organisation, for example companies, clubs and societies, have some sort of basic rules about how they are to be run. This would include information about who has the power to take decisions, whether and how those decisions must be approved by the members of the organisation and the other rights of those members. These rules are commonly called the constitution of that organisation.

Similarly, a country would have a constitution. This would state who has the power to govern that country, how they were chosen and the powers that they possessed. The idea is that the constitution would be generally accepted by the people of that country and therefore grant legitimacy to whatever the system of government was in that country. The constitution should limit the power of government and give protection to the rights and liberties of the people of that country.

Key term: constitution

The system of government and the collection of rules that establish and regulate it.

Written and unwritten constitutions

Nearly every country in the world has a **written constitution**, sometimes called a **codified constitution**. This is a document that sets out the government framework in that country, the organs of government and their powers. It could be a short or lengthy document, as different countries make different choices, but *the important point* is that the constitution has a higher legal status than the ordinary law. Many countries would make a distinction between *public law* that relates to the written constitution and *private law* that relates to ordinary citizens in areas such as contract and tort. It is common to have different courts for public and private law and even a high-level, specialist court to interpret the constitution, such as the Supreme Court in the USA. There is usually a special procedure to change the constitution, such as a two-thirds majority of the legislature or a referendum.

Key term: written (or codified) constitution

A document with a special legal status that sets out the system of government and the collection of rules that establish and regulate it.

Contents of a constitution

Written constitutions vary in size and content, but they would contain some or all of the following features:

1. A statement that this is what the 'people' want.
2. A statement of the values important to that country.
3. An organisation chart of government setting out the executive (government), legislature (law making) and judicial (deciding legal disputes) functions.
4. Electoral procedure.
5. The structure of the state, specifically whether it is unitary or federal in nature.
6. Procedures to change the constitution.
7. A Bill of Rights that protects the liberties and freedoms of the people of that state.
8. Protections for minority groups.

The UK has an unwritten constitution

The UK is unusual because it does not have a written constitution. The reasons for this are historical. Countries adopt written constitutions when there is a dramatic break with the past, such as overthrowing the previous form of government, defeat in war, economic collapse or the gaining of independence. None of these have occurred in modern times in the UK, so the system of government has evolved over the centuries. Despite the absence of a constitutional document, the UK does have a clear and generally accepted system of government, so it does have a constitution.

The UK constitution is evolutionary

The UK constitution has developed and changed over the centuries. The powers of the King or Queen, Parliament and the prime minister have all changed since those institutions came into existence. Once the monarch was the most important person in the constitution, now it is the prime minister.

Much of the UK constitution can be found in Acts of Parliament and is therefore legally binding, but in contrast to a written constitution,

Acts of Parliament that have constitutional effect are no different from any other Act of Parliament and there is no special procedure to repeal them. For example, Parliament passed the European Communities Act 1972 in order to join the European Union (EU) and could repeal it in the EU (Withdrawal) Act 2018, so that the UK could leave. Although a referendum was held in 2016 to ask the electorate whether they wanted to leave the EU, as explained in *R (Miller) v Secretary of State for Exiting the European Union* [2017] UKSC 5, there was no constitutional or legal requirement to do this. All that was required to change one Act of Parliament was another Act of Parliament (see **Chapter 9** for more information about the EU).

Human rights were not legally protected within the UK until the Human Rights Act 1998. Although under s 3 of that Act legislation must be interpreted in accordance with that Act, there is nothing to stop Parliament passing laws that infringe human rights or, indeed, repealing the Human Rights Act.

Much of the UK constitution is not law at all but is made up of **conventions**. These are understandings, habits or practices that regulate how members of the government behave. In other words, they are the accepted way of doing things, which most people respect. Conventions mean that the constitution is very adaptable and can change according to the circumstances. Have a look at **Practice example 1.1** for an illustration of this.

Practice example 1.1

A new prime minister has just been elected and wants the UK to rejoin the EU. The prime minister thinks that she must hold a referendum to gain approval for this course of action. Is the prime minister correct?

There is no *legal* requirement to do so, because there is not a written constitution that requires this procedure for constitutional change. There may be a *political* problem in not holding a referendum if the electorate expect it.

Revision tip

Just because the UK does not have a written constitution it does not mean that there are no constitutional rules. There definitely are rules, which you need to learn and remember for the SQE assessment.

Federal or unitary constitutions

In a federal state, the **federal constitution** divides power between a central government and the governments of the different regions of that country. For example, the USA has a federal government and each of the 50 states also has its own government. As the name suggests, the UK is a union of once independent countries, namely England, Scotland, Wales and Northern Ireland, but a federal structure was not adopted. Instead, it is a **unitary constitution**, where the ultimate sovereign power is retained by the central government based in Westminster. In particular, the UK Parliament retains sovereignty, which is the power to enact any law that it chooses. These Acts of Parliament override any other kinds of law. In contrast, the legislature of a federal state usually cannot override the written constitution or the legislative powers allocated to the regions.

Key term: federal constitution

A system of government in which the authority to govern is divided between a central government and regions, provinces or states.

Key term: unitary constitution

A system of government in which the authority to govern is concentrated in the central government.

From 1998 onwards, the UK Parliament began a process of devolution, granting powers of self-government to Scotland, Wales and Northern Ireland. However, the UK Parliament was careful to retain sovereignty and can override the wishes of the devolved countries, as indicated in *R (Miller) v Secretary of State for Exiting the European Union* [2017] UKSC 5. Only the Parliament of the UK needed to legislate to leave the EU. The consent of the legislatures of Scotland and Northern Ireland was not required. Have a look at **Practice example 1.2** for an illustration of this (see **Chapter 3, page 49** for more about devolution).

Practice example 1.2

The prime minister wants to abolish the Scottish Parliament. Can he do this?

Legally yes, if the Parliament of the UK passes an Act of Parliament to do so. An Act of the UK Parliament, the Scotland Act 2016, states that the Scottish Parliament and the Scottish government are permanent parts of the UK constitution, but this Act can be repealed. This neatly illustrates the difference between the UK unitary constitution and a federal constitution.

Table 1.1: Written constitutions versus UK unwritten constitution

Written constitutions	UK unwritten constitution
Special procedure to change	All constitutional rules can be changed
Most countries have one	UK is unusual
Rights are protected under the constitution	Specific legislation to protect rights
Constitutional rules can be found in one document	Constitutional rules can be found in Acts of Parliament, cases and conventions
Better control over government	Government has freedom to act
Constitutional court enforces the constitution	Constitutional cases are heard in the ordinary courts
Written constitution might not be obeyed	Tradition respected
Written constitution cannot contain every rule	Conventions, cases and Acts of Parliament provide more constitutional rules
The constitution may divide power between federal and state governments	The UK (Westminster) Parliament retains supreme power (sovereignty)

Summary: constitutions	
WHAT is a constitution?	The rules under which a country is governed.
WHEN is it used?	All the time, but it is particularly relevant when there is a dispute about the rights of the government or citizens.
WHO is it used by?	The government and all the citizens of that country.

THE SOURCES OF THE CONSTITUTION

The constitution of the UK cannot be found in one constitutional document but has various sources. This section will give an overview of the following sources:

• Acts of Parliament
• case law
• the **royal prerogative**

- historical documents
- the law and custom of Parliament
- EU law
- constitutional theories.

Acts of Parliament

Much of the UK constitution is written down and legally enforceable as it is contained in Acts of Parliament. In contrast to a written constitution, these Acts can be easily amended or repealed, simply by passing another Act of Parliament. Many of the most important parts of the constitution can be found in Acts of Parliament. **Table 1.2** gives a few examples, which you will see later in the book.

Table 1.2: Constitutionally important Acts of Parliament

Act of Settlement 1700	This provides for the royal succession and lays down who is entitled to be King or Queen (see **Chapter 4, page 62**).
Act of Union 1706	Two independent countries, England and Scotland, joined to form Great Britain and the Parliaments of England and Scotland were dissolved and merged into one, new Parliament (see **Chapter 3, page 49**).
Parliament Acts 1911 and 1949	Although these two Acts do not set out the powers of Parliament, they do restrict the power of the House of Lords. The elected House of Commons became the superior House and the Lords may only delay legislation passed by the Commons for one year (see **Chapter 2, page 24**).
Human Rights Act 1998	This Act allowed victims of a breach of human rights to enforce the provisions of the European Convention on Human Rights (ECHR) in the courts of the UK (see **Chapter 8, page 134**).
Constitutional Reform Act 2005	The Act established the Supreme Court and provided for a separation of powers in the UK constitution (see **Chapter 1, page 12**).
European Communities Act 1972	Under this Act, the UK joined the EU (then known as the European Economic Communities) and allowed EU law to be enforced in the courts of the UK (see **Chapter 9, page 157**).
EU (Withdrawal) Act 2018	Under this Act the UK left the EU. Although EU Law (now known as 'retained law') remains in force in the UK, it no longer has supremacy over UK law (see **Chapter 9, page 159**).

Case law

Many countries have specialist constitutional courts, such as the Supreme Court in the USA. The UK does not, and a constitutional issue may be tried in any level of court. Under the precedent system, the decisions of the House of Lords and its successor, the Supreme Court, are the most authoritative. The Supreme Court of the USA has the power to overrule unconstitutional laws, but the UK Supreme Court does not. Despite that, as the constitution is unwritten many constitutional issues can only be decided in court. The fundamental principle of the constitution, parliamentary sovereignty, can only be found in court decisions. **Table 1.3** shows some examples of constitutionally important court decisions.

Table 1.3: Constitutionally important court decisions

Pickin v British Rail Board [1974] AC 765	The House of Lords concluded that Parliament was the supreme authority in the constitution and a court could neither investigate nor question an Act passed by Parliament.
R v Secretary of State for Transport, ex parte Factortame No 2 [1991] 1 AC 603	After joining the EU, the House of Lords had to reconsider the question of parliamentary supremacy. Their Lordships concluded that the European Communities Act 1972 had given the EU authority to legislate for the UK and given permission for EU law to have supremacy over UK Acts of Parliament.
R (Miller) v Secretary of State for Exiting the European Union [2017] UKSC 5	The Supreme Court concluded that leaving the EU could not be done by using the royal prerogative, because only another Act of Parliament could repeal the European Communities Act 1972.

The royal prerogative

The monarch retains legal powers to enable him to rule the country, which is known as the royal prerogative. Some originate from ancient Acts of Parliament, but others are powers that have always been claimed and are therefore part of the common law. Sometimes, the existence and extent of these powers is disputed and then the courts might be called upon to adjudicate. For example, the King has the power to summon, dissolve or prorogue (suspend) Parliament, but nowadays the convention is that this is done on the advice of the prime minister. *R (Miller) v Prime Minister* [2019] UKSC 41 decided that Parliament fulfilled a vital constitutional role and could not therefore be suspended for longer than a short period of time.

The prime minister or other senior government minister decide upon the use of the King's legal powers and exercise these powers in his name. The established practice (convention) is that the King must be consulted. He can express agreement or disagreement with the prime minister's chosen course of action, but ultimately would not refuse (see **Chapter 4, page 62**).

Key term: royal prerogative

The remaining royal powers of government.

Historic documents

The two main historical sources are:
- Magna Carta 1215
- The Bill of Rights 1689.

Magna Carta 1215

The significance of this charter is that King John agreed that his powers were not unlimited and that his subjects did have certain rights. It could be regarded as the ancestor of written constitutions, but even though it was turned into an Act of Parliament in 1297, it is of little practical significance today and its provisions would not be enforceable in a court. Clause 39, which stated that a freeman should be tried for crimes by 'his peers', could be regarded as a recognition of jury trials and clause 40 guarantees a right to justice. At most, these might be regarded as underlying constitutional principles.

The Bill of Rights 1689

James II fled England in 1688 during events described as the Glorious Revolution and was replaced by King William and Queen Mary. Parliament laid down the terms under which they would rule in the Bill of Rights, which was later given statutory force by Parliament. The importance of this document is that Parliament was now the supreme authority in England, not the King or Queen. Parliament, not the monarch, would make the laws, raise taxes and authorise the keeping of an army.

The law and custom of Parliament

As it is the supreme authority in the constitution, Parliament makes its own laws about its procedures and its members' behaviour. Article 9 of the Bill of Rights recognised freedom of speech in Parliament and the courts accepted that they could not rule on parliamentary procedure in *Pickin v British Rail Board* [1974] AC 765. This area of law is known as parliamentary privilege (see **Chapter 2, page 30** for parliamentary privilege).

EU law

This might once have been regarded as a separate source of constitutional law for the UK, but the EU (Withdrawal Act) 2018 makes clear that retained EU law only has force in the UK because an Act of Parliament allows it to do so and subsequent Acts may alter that law (see **Chapter 9, page 159**).

CONSTITUTIONAL THEORIES

You need to know about constitutional theories (**Figure 1.1**) because they are the underlying principles behind many court decisions. They are particularly relevant when we look at judicial review (see **Chapter 7**).

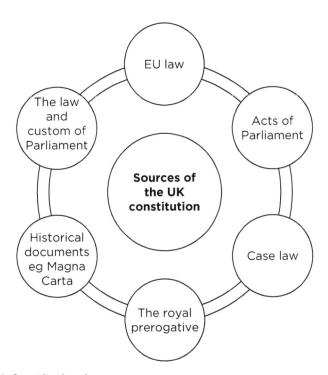

Figure 1.1: Constitutional sources

The separation of powers

Simply put, this means that no one person or body should hold all the powers of government, otherwise there would be a tyranny or dictatorship. The best-known version of this theory is that of Montesquieu, who wrote that there were three main functions of government and that they should be exercised by three separate bodies:

- the legislative or law making
- executive or law applying
- judicial or law enforcing.

The USA constitution is based on Montesquieu's theory, where under Article 1 the legislative branch are the elected Houses of Congress, under Article 2 the executive branch is the separately elected president and under Article 3 the judicial branch is the Supreme Court, which is able to overturn unconstitutional legislation.

The UK does not have this system, as the legislature and executive are mixed. The elected House of Commons and the appointed and hereditary House of Lords form the legislature, Parliament. The conventions are that the executive, which is the prime minister and his/her ministers, must be members of the Commons or Lords and that they must have a majority in the House of Commons. Yet there is some separation, in that there are only about 120 government ministers and they are heavily outnumbered by the rest of the legislature, which hold them to account. The judiciary are, however, separate and maintain their independence from Parliament. Parliament makes the law, but judges decide what it means when they apply it in court cases.

The rule of law

Even the rulers or government of a country must obey the law. In the UK, a nineteenth-century English writer, AV Dicey, developed an influential version of this theory. There were three main principles:

- *All government actions should be authorised by the law*. Government officials could not interfere with the liberty of a person, unless the law allowed it. The government should not possess wide, discretionary powers.
- *There should be equality before the law*. There should be the same laws and courts for everyone, including the government. The government should not have immunities from the law.
- *The courts would protect individual liberty*. Anyone could apply to the courts and the judges would uphold liberty against the claims of government.

The importance of an independent judiciary can be found in both these theories and they received some recognition in the Constitutional Reform Act 2005. Have a look at **Practice example 1.3** for an illustration of this.

Practice example 1.3

The secretary of state for justice wants claimants before employment tribunals to pay the full cost of their hearing, so that these tribunals are self-financing. Would this be legal?

On the face of it, yes, if the secretary of state used the correct legislative procedure to change court fees. However, this would be contrary to the second rule of law principle. Access to the courts is a fundamental constitutional principle and a judicial review of this decision would be successful.

Revision tip

The separation of powers and the rule of law are quite often confused. The independence of the judges is important in both theories, but remember that these are two different theories.

CONVENTIONS

Much of the UK constitution is not law at all, but just the established and accepted way of doing things. For your revision, it is important to understand what conventions are and how to identify them.

What are conventions?

The nineteenth-century constitutional writer Dicey popularised the ideas of conventions, understandings and practices. Many of the most important parts of the constitution are only governed by convention. There is no law that says that there must be a prime minister, how he or she should be chosen or the extent of his or her power. Every prime minister has an inner group of ministers, called the Cabinet, but this is not required by law either. The King retains considerable legal powers, but these are only exercised on the advice of the prime minister. Legally, the King could refuse the royal assent to a Bill presented by Parliament, but the convention is that he would never do so. Similarly, the King commands the armed forces, but the prime minister or secretary of state for defence decides upon their deployment.

Key term: conventions
Non-legal rules of the constitution.

Identifying conventions?

Nowadays, many conventions have been written down. The Ministerial Code lays down detailed rules for the conduct of government and ministers, but it is not an Act of Parliament and so is not legally enforceable. However, many conventions have not been officially written down and there can be disagreement about the existence and scope of some conventions. The constitutional writer, Ivor Jennings, did not believe that this was a problem and that conventions laid down clear constitutional rules. The existence of a convention could be determined by applying a three-stage test.

Namely, are there precedents?
- Has this situation occurred before and what happened?
- Did the people involved think that there was a rule that compelled them to act that way?
- Is there a reason for this rule, in other words does it fit in with the rest of the constitution?

This works well for a convention where there is a clearly established pattern of behaviour, such as the King and royal assent, but less well with ministerial misconduct, where the situations in which a minister should resign are constantly changing.

Enforcement of conventions

A bigger question is how can conventions be enforced if they are not law? The courts will not enforce them, as shown with the convention of Cabinet confidentiality in *Attorney General v Jonathan Cape* [1976] QB 752. Dicey thought that conventions would be obeyed because of the political difficulties that breaking them would cause. It is the convention to summon Parliament every year and if this did not happen taxation could not be authorised nor could the keeping of an army. Perhaps the best explanation of the workings of convention comes from a Canadian case, *Reference re Amendment of the Constitution of Canada* (1982) 125 DLR (3d) 1. Canada has a written constitution, but it also has conventions. In this case, the court stated that conventions are like morality and reflect the constitutional values of the period.

People obey conventions because they think that it is right thing to do, so enforcement is not usually necessary. If it is, the sanction is political. A constitutional superior could dismiss the convention breaker. For example, the prime minister can sack ministers and ultimately the King could require the prime minister to resign. As with morality, the opinion of others might enforce obedience to the conventional rules. A misbehaving government minister would face the disapproval of his colleagues and maybe the rest of Parliament. Public opinion might also ensure compliance, as ultimately governments must face elections. Have a look at **Practice example 1.4** for an illustration of this.

Practice example 1.4

The prime minister has been recently elected with a large majority in the House of Commons but has been behaving in an eccentric manner, which is very unpopular with the public. Can the King dismiss him from office?

Legally yes, because under the royal prerogative the King appoints the prime minister. However, the convention is that while the prime minister maintains a majority in the House of Commons they remain in office. If the prime minister lost that majority and yet refused to resign, the prime minister would break that convention and, as a last resort, the King could use his legal power to dismiss.

Although the courts cannot enforce conventions, because they are not the law and might even contradict the strict legal position, they certainly recognise their existence and conventions can influence their judgments. This can be seen in *R (Miller) v Prime Minister* [2019] UKSC 41, where the convention of ministerial accountability to Parliament was accepted as a vital part of the constitution. If the prime minister could prorogue (suspend) Parliament there would be no accountability. Therefore, the court concluded that there was no legal power under the prerogative to suspend Parliament for over a month.

Exam warning

The constitution consists of both laws and conventions. When you are asked a question, you will be asked about the constitutional position. As in **Practice example 1.4**, conventions may modify the law. Your answer should be what the convention says.

Summary: conventions	
WHAT is a convention?	They are the non-legal rules of the constitution.
WHEN are they used?	When there is no legal rule, or the legal rule is out of date.
WHO are they used by?	The King, government minsters, members of Parliament and civil servants.

■ KEY POINT CHECKLIST

This chapter has covered the following key knowledge points. You can use these to structure your revision, making sure to recall the key details for each point, as covered in this chapter.

- Countries have constitutions because there need to be rules about how that country is governed.
- In a written constitution the constitutional rules are contained in a document of higher legal status. In an unwritten constitution the constitutional rules are found in different sources.
- The minimum contents of a constitution would be an organisation chart of government.
- In a federal constitution power is divided between a central and regional governments. In a unitary constitution power is concentrated in the central government.
- The UK constitution can be found in Acts of Parliament, cases and conventions.
- Constitutional conventions fill the gaps not covered by Acts of Parliament or cases.

■ KEY TERMS AND CONCEPTS

- constitution (**page 3**)
- written or codified constitution (**page 4**)
- federal constitution (**page 6**)
- unitary constitution (**page 6**)
- royal prerogative (**page 10**)
- conventions (**page 14**)

■ SQE1-STYLE QUESTIONS

QUESTION 1

The government wants to repeal the Human Rights Act 1998. The [fictitious] Human Rights (Repeal) Bill has been passed by the Commons by a large majority. The House of Lords, however, has rejected the Bill, also by a large majority.

Which of the following best describes the legal position in this case?

A. It is not possible to repeal the Human Rights Act 1998 because that would breach an international treaty, the European Convention on Human Rights.

B. The government must obtain royal assent.

C. The government must obtain consent from the House of Lords.

D. The government must pass the Bill through the Commons again.

E. The government must wait a year and then pass the Bill through the Commons again.

QUESTION 2

The Scottish Parliament votes to reduce the rate of income tax in that country. The UK government disagrees with this course of action.

Which of the following best describes the course of action the UK government can take to stop this?

A. Negotiate with the Scottish government.

B. Use the royal prerogative.

C. Nothing, the Scottish Parliament has the power to legislate on this subject.

D. Pass a UK Act of Parliament.

E. Order the Scottish government not to do this.

QUESTION 3

The Lord Chancellor is obligated by law to uphold the independence of the judiciary. A judge has been much criticised in the media for a controversial decision he has made. The Lord Chief Justice (LCJ) wants the Lord Chancellor to defend the judge, but the Lord Chancellor declines.

What options are available to the Lord Chancellor?

A. The LCJ may seek a judicial review to compel the Lord Chancellor to act.

B. The LCJ may only seek to criticise the Lord Chancellor.

C. The LCJ can do nothing, as the Lord Chancellor is his constitutional superior.

D. The LCJ can do nothing, as the Lord Chancellor decides the meaning of an Act.

E. The LCJ can do nothing, as the obligation owed by the Lord Chancellor is too vague to enforce.

QUESTION 4

A client who has been accused of speeding approaches a solicitor for legal advice. He is to be tried in the magistrates' court for this alleged offence, but he claims that he has a constitutional right under Magna Carta to trial by jury.

What advice should the solicitor give him?

A. Magna Carta has been repealed, so trial by jury is no longer guaranteed.

B. Magna Carta is a document with no legal effect.

C. Speeding is governed by road traffic legislation.

D. All constitutional rights are subject to exceptions.

E. The UK does not have a written constitution guaranteeing rights.

QUESTION 5

The Supreme Court has decided that a certain category of self-employed people are not liable to pay income tax. The government is concerned because there are thousands of people in this category and there will be a major loss of tax revenue.

What is the best course of action that the government could take?

A. Appeal the decision to the Court of Justice of the EU.

B. Appeal the decision to the European Court of Human Rights.

C. Order the Justices of the Supreme Court to change their decision.

D. Use Parliament to pass an Act amending the tax law.

E. Accept the decision of the Supreme Court.

■ ANSWERS TO QUESTIONS

Answers to 'What do you know already?' questions at the start of the chapter

1) Every country, even dictatorships, need some rules on how they are governed.
2) False. The constitution of a country is laid down in a document that has higher legal status than the ordinary law. An ordinary Act of Parliament could not do this.
3) The reasons are historical. The UK has not had a revolution or gained independence in modern times.
4) In a federal state, government powers are divided between central and regional government. In a unitary state, government powers are concentrated in central government.
5) Yes. Most of the constitution is contained in Acts of Parliament.
6) The correct answer was (b). The royal prerogative is the legal power of the King, but by convention it is exercised, on his behalf, by His Majesty's government. The King has immunity from the law, but not the rest of his family.
7) The correct answer was (b). Conventions are non-legal customs and practices, under which a country is governed. Convention is another name for an international treaty, but that is not the same as a constitutional convention.

Answers to end-of-chapter SQE1-style questions

Question 1:
   The correct answer was E. If the House of Lords disagrees with the House of Commons, this is the procedure required by the Parliament Acts 1911 and 1949. All Acts of Parliament may be repealed, even important constitutional Acts.

Question 2:
   The correct answer was D. Although the Scottish Parliament has the power to change the income tax rate under the Scotland Act 2012, the UK Parliament has sovereignty and can overrule it.

Question 3:
   The correct answer was B. This is because the guarantee of judicial independence is not specific enough to be enforced in the courts. But it does lay down a principle that could be used as a basis of criticism.

Question 4:

> The correct answer was C. This is because although Magna Carta is an Act of Parliament, all Acts of Parliament can be repealed or amended by later Acts of Parliament.

Question 5:

> The correct answer was D. This is because Parliament has sovereignty and can change any law it wants, including decisions by the highest court.

■ KEY CASES, RULES, STATUTES AND INSTRUMENTS

The SQE1 Assessment Specification does not require you to remember the names of these two cases and the statute, but the principles contained in them are important:

- *R (Miller) v Secretary of State for Exiting the European Union* [2017] UKSC 5.
- *R (Miller) v Prime Minister* [2019] UKSC 41.
- Constitutional Reform Act 2005.

2

Parliament: Parliamentary sovereignty and parliamentary privilege

■ MAKE SURE YOU KNOW

This chapter covers parliamentary sovereignty, parliamentary privilege and the main functions of parliament that you will need to know and be able to apply to problems and situations for your SQE1 assessment.

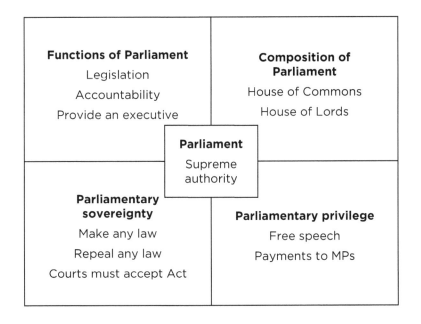

Functions of Parliament
Legislation
Accountability
Provide an executive

Composition of Parliament
House of Commons
House of Lords

Parliament
Supreme authority

Parliamentary sovereignty
Make any law
Repeal any law
Courts must accept Act

Parliamentary privilege
Free speech
Payments to MPs

■ SQE ASSESSMENT ADVICE

As you work through this chapter, remember to pay particular attention in your revision to:
- Parliament's claim to supreme authority in the UK constitution
- the courts' acceptance of that claim
- courts do not question Acts of Parliament
- Parliament can make any law that it wants
- Parliament can change any law that it wants
- the courts' acceptance of Parliament's power to regulate its own proceedings and own members.

■ WHAT DO YOU KNOW ALREADY?

Have a go at these questions before reading this chapter. If you find some difficult or cannot remember the answers, make a note to look more closely at that subtopic during your revision.

1) An Act of Parliament is made by the House of Commons and the House of Lords. True or false?
   [The Parliament Acts 1911 and 1949, page 24]
2) Which of the following can an Act of Parliament *not* do?
   a) break international law
   b) legislate on any subject
   c) prevent a law from being changed.
   [Parliamentary sovereignty, page 25]
3) An Act of Parliament may contain a special procedure (eg two-thirds majority), referendum, for its repeal. True or false?
   [Special procedures, page 27]
4) Which of the following is correct? European Union (EU) law had supremacy over an Act of Parliament because:
   a) the EU claimed this right
   b) a UK Act of Parliament permitted it
   c) the Supreme Court agreed.
   [Parliamentary sovereignty and the EU, page 29]
5) Under what circumstances can a Member of Parliament (MP) be prosecuted?
   [Enforcement of breaches of privilege, page 35]
6) Which of the following is correct? A media report of a debate in Parliament:
   a) is completely protected from a defamation action
   b) has no protection from a defamation action
   c) is protected from a defamation action if it is fair and accurate.
   [Publication of parliamentary proceedings, page 32]

PARLIAMENTARY FUNCTIONS

This section enables you to revise the functions of and the relationship between the two Houses of Parliament:
• the House of Commons
• the House of Lords
• the Parliament Acts.

Parliament came into existence in 1265 and gradually became the dominant part of the government. As the UK has an unwritten constitution, there is no single document or Act of Parliament that sets out the powers of Parliament, but the Bill of Rights 1689 made clear that Parliament was now the supreme power in the country, taking over from the King or Queen.

Nowadays Parliament:
• enacts legislation (acts as a legislature)
• authorises taxation and government expenditure
• provides the government (executive)
• holds the executive to account for its conduct of government
• represents the people and secures redress of their grievances.

Parliament consists of two separate chambers, the House of Commons and the House of Lords.

The House of Commons

England, Scotland, Wales and Northern Ireland are divided up into 650 parliamentary constituencies, each of which elect an MP to the House of Commons. MPs are elected under the first-past-the-post (majoritarian) system. According to the Fixed-Term Parliaments Act 2011, a general election must be held every five years. British citizens, citizens of the Republic of Ireland and Commonwealth citizens, with a right to remain in the UK, can vote from the age of 18. However, they must register to vote in the constituency where they reside or have a local connection.

The House of Lords

Originally, all the members of the House of Lords held a hereditary peerage. The Life Peerages Act 1958 allowed the prime minister to appoint Lords for their lifetime only, with no right of inheritance for their heirs. The House of Lords Act 1999 removed most of the hereditary Lords. Those Lords now elect 90 of their group to continue as members of the House of Lords. The 26 most senior bishops of the Church of England are also members of the House of Lords. The 680 life peers are by far the biggest group in the Lords, which has a total of 792 members. Have a look at **Practice example 2.1** for an illustration of this.

Practice example 2.1

Horace has just become the Duke of Whatnot, after the death of his father, and wants to take up his father's seat in the House of Lords. Can he do this?

No. Historically he would have done so, subject to the House of Lords determining whether his claim to the title was valid. Now, however, he would have to be elected by the existing hereditary peers in the Lords.

The Parliament Acts 1911 and 1949

An Act of Parliament is normally passed by both the House of Commons and the House of Lords and then receives the royal assent (see **Chapter 5** for details of this procedure).

By the nineteenth century, it was accepted that the House of Commons was the dominant House of Parliament, because it was democratically elected. The Parliament Acts put this into law. The House of Lords cannot reject a parliamentary Bill passed by the House of Commons, but only delay it from becoming an Act. The Parliament Act 1911 had a delaying power of two years, but the 1949 Act reduced this to one year between the second reading in the first session and the third reading in the second session. The House of Commons must pass the Bill twice and this gives them time to reflect upon public opinion and whether the Bill is necessary. The Parliament Acts procedure is rarely used, because the two Houses agree upon a compromise. The Parliament Acts procedure cannot be used to extend the life of Parliament, which is fixed at five years. The House of Lords has to accept 'money Bills', involving taxation or expenditure, within one month.

An Act passed under the Parliament Acts, without the agreement of the House of Lords, is just as valid as any other Act of Parliament and cannot be challenged in the courts: *R (Jackson) v Attorney General* [2006] 1 AC 262.

Summary: parliamentary functions

WHAT is Parliament?	It is the elected House of Commons and the appointed House of Lords.
WHAT does it do?	It makes the law, provides an executive and holds that executive to account.
WHO is in charge?	The House of Commons is the dominant House and may legislate without the consent of the House of Lords.

PARLIAMENTARY SOVEREIGNTY

You may be asked in SQE1 about whether an Act of Parliament could ever be invalid. This section enables you to revise the different aspects of **parliamentary sovereignty**, namely:

- the validity of an Act of Parliament
- repeal
- special procedures
- devolution
- parliamentary sovereignty and the EU
- the Human Rights Act 1998.

The theory goes that every developed state must have a supreme authority, known as the sovereign, which has supreme power in that state. This means that the sovereign has the power to make laws that are obeyed and unchallenged. AV Dicey, writing in 1885, popularised this idea and identified the sovereign as 'the Queen in Parliament'. What he meant was that legislation had to be agreed by the House of Commons, House of Lords and the Queen or King. Parliamentary sovereignty means that:

- Parliament has the right to make or unmake any law.
- No person or body can override or set aside laws made by Parliament.
- No Parliament can bind a future Parliament.
- Parliament does not share the right to make law with any other person or body.

Parliament has claimed this supremacy since the Glorious Revolution of 1688, when one King was overthrown and replaced with another, chosen by Parliament. The Bill of Rights 1689 proclaimed Parliament's supremacy and it has been accepted ever since. This principle has been described as a 'political fact'. It would only change if there was another revolution and a new way of legislating was generally accepted.

Key term: parliamentary sovereignty

Parliament is the supreme legal authority in the UK that can create or end any law. The courts cannot overrule its legislation and no Parliament can pass laws that future Parliaments cannot change.

The validity of an Act of Parliament

In particular, the judiciary have accepted the supremacy of Parliament and so attempts to challenge the validity of Acts of Parliament in court have failed. See **Table 2.1** for examples.

Repeal

All Acts of Parliament may be repealed by a later Act of Parliament, even if the wording of the earlier Act suggests that it cannot.

Express repeal

The new Act will mention the older Act and specify the older Act, or the parts of the older Act, which are no longer the law.

Table 2.1: The courts will not question the validity of an Act of Parliament

Mortensen v Peters (1906) SCLR 872	It was alleged that an Act of Parliament was contrary to international law, but the court dismissed these claims as irrelevant.
Cheney v Conn [1968] 1 All ER 779, 782	It was alleged that an Act of Parliament was contrary to international law, but the judge explained: 'What the statute itself enacts cannot be unlawful, because what the statute says and provides is itself the law, and the highest form of law that is known to this country.'
British Coal Corporation v The King [1935] AC 500	An Act of Parliament had granted the British colony Canada, independence, but Parliament could still legislate for Canada if it wished and the British courts would uphold this as the law.
Pickin v British Rail Board [1974] AC	Pickin alleged that Parliament had not followed its own procedures, failing to notify him of a Bill that affected him. The court refused to investigate the claim. Parliament decided its own procedures.

Implied repeal

If two Acts of Parliament contradict each other, the later Act is the law. In *Ellen Street Estates v Minister of Health* [1934] KB 590, a 1919 Act of Parliament referred to other Acts and stated that 'so far as inconsistent with this Act, those provisions shall cease to have or shall not have effect'. These words repealed Acts *earlier* than 1919, but could not stop the 1919 Act itself being repealed by *later* Acts of Parliament.

Implied repeal not possible

In more recent times the courts have asserted that some Acts of Parliament, of fundamental, constitutional importance, could not be impliedly repealed, but could only be expressly repealed:

*   *Thoburn v Sunderland City Council* [2002] 1 CMLR 50. Laws LJ stated that the European Communities Act 1972 could not be impliedly repealed by a 1985 Act of Parliament that might appear to contradict it. The European Communities Act 1972 could only be repealed by clear, unambiguous, express words. Other Acts of constitutional importance that could not be impliedly repealed included Magna Carta, the Bill of Rights 1689, the Act of Union 1707, the Reform Acts that extended the right to vote, the Scotland Act 1998 and the Government of Wales Act 1998.
*   The Supreme Court accepted that the Bill of Rights 1689 could not be impliedly repealed in *R (HS2 Action Alliance Ltd) v Secretary of State for Transport* [2014] UKSC 3.

Revision tip

When revising, try to understand these theoretical arguments against the unlimited supremacy of Parliament but remember that the courts have rejected these claims.

Special procedures

It is common in written constitutions to specify a special procedure, such as a two-thirds majority of the legislature or a referendum of the electorate, to change certain parts of the constitution. Because it is generally believed that one Parliament cannot bind another, such procedures are rare in UK Acts of Parliament, but not unknown. For example, the Northern Ireland Act 1998 provides that a referendum must approve any change to the constitutional status of Northern Ireland. Would an Act changing the status of Northern Ireland be invalid if no referendum was held? There are cases from Commonwealth countries that support this idea.

In the Commonwealth

Attorney General for New South Wales v Trethowan [1932] AC 526
The legislature of New South Wales (NSW) passed an Act holding that their upper house, the Legislative Council, could not be abolished without the approval of a referendum. Later, the legislature abolished the council, without holding a referendum. A UK Act of Parliament gave full powers to the legislature to make laws if they had been passed in the 'manner and form' laid down by the law in force in that country. On that basis, the Privy Council decided that the legislature of NSW must respect the procedure laid down in its own earlier legislation and, as they had not held the referendum, the new law was invalid.

In the UK

It is unlikely that the above ruling would apply to the UK as the legislature of NSW was not a sovereign body. It was given its powers by a UK Act of Parliament. The Fixed-Term Parliaments Act 2011 states that a general election can only be held every five years. A two-third majority of the House of Commons must agree to an earlier election. This was easily bypassed by the Early Parliamentary Elections Act 2019, passed with a simple majority, stating the date when the next general election would be held. Have a look at **Practice example 2.2** for an illustration of this.

Practice example 2.2

Because of difficulties in implementing the Northern Ireland Protocol after withdrawal from the EU, Parliament is planning to pass an Act allowing Northern Ireland to leave the UK. There are no plans to hold a referendum. Can Parliament do this?

Legally, Parliament can, as it is not bound by the provisions of the Northern Ireland Act 1998. Politically, it would be unwise, because it would be unpopular with some of the population of Northern Ireland.

Devolution

The UK Parliament passed Acts of Parliament granting powers of self-government and the ability to make their own laws on certain matters to Scotland, Wales and Northern Ireland. All three Acts were careful to state that the UK Parliament retained supremacy. This means that the

UK Parliament can take back the powers that were devolved. In *R (Miller) v Secretary of State for Exiting the EU* [2017], the Scotland Act 2016 and the Wales Act 2017 gave statutory force to the Sewel Convention that the UK Parliament would not legislate on devolved matters without the consent of the Scottish Parliament or Welsh Assembly. Parliamentary sovereignty meant that the UK Parliament could disregard the wishes of Scottish and Irish governments in the process of leaving the EU, even taking back some devolved powers. **Practice example 2.3** illustrates how this works.

Practice example 2.3

As part of its planning for epidemics of serious disease, the UK government wants to have the same laws on public health throughout the UK. The governments of Scotland and Wales strongly object, because health is a matter devolved to their Parliaments. Can the UK Parliament make these laws?

The *Miller* case, above, makes clear that, legally, the UK Parliament can override the wishes of the legislatures of Scotland and Wales.

Parliamentary sovereignty and the EU

The UK joined what was then called the European Communities in 1973. The European Communities Act 1972 stated that EU law became part of the law of the UK and should be enforced in UK courts. Section 2(4) required that UK Acts of Parliament should be interpreted in accordance with EU law see **Table 2.2**.

The European Union Withdrawal Act 2018 expressly repealed the ECA 1972. The EU can no longer legislate for the UK (see **Chapter 9, page 159**).

Table 2.2: The status of EU law in the UK

R v Secretary of State for Transport ex parte Factortame [1991] 1 AC 603	The House of Lords decided that sovereignty had been 'loaned' to the EU. While the 1972 Act was in force, UK Acts should be interpreted so as not to conflict with EU law. If that could not be done, as in this case, EU law would override the UK Act.
Thoburn v Sunderland City Council [2002] 1 CMLR 50	The European Communities Act 1972 could only be expressly repealed

The Human Rights Act 1998

Under this Act, the rights protected by the European Convention on Human Rights could be enforced in UK courts. There is nothing to protect this Act from being repealed or amended, but s 3 requires that Acts of Parliament 'must be read and given effect in a way which is compatible with the Convention rights' (see **Chapter 8** for more details).

Human rights and statutory interpretation

This principle has been extended beyond the strict requirements of the Human Rights Act 1998. The courts also interpret Acts so that they do not contravene fundamental principles of the constitution, such as access to the courts in R (Unison) v Lord Chancellor [2017] UKSC 51 and the independence of the judiciary from the executive in R (Evans) v Attorney General [2015] UKSC 21. However, if an Act of Parliament expressly restricts a human right, the courts must comply with the wishes of Parliament.

Summary: parliamentary sovereignty	
WHAT is parliamentary sovereignty?	The right of Parliament to make any law that it wants.
WHO says so?	Parliament asserts this right and the courts have accepted it.

PARLIAMENTARY PRIVILEGE

As the supreme body in the UK constitution, Parliament regulates its own proceedings. It controls the conduct of its own members and has the power to punish those who break its rules. This is known as **parliamentary privilege**. Knowledge of parliamentary privilege is required for SQE1 and this section will help you revise how it works:

• freedom of speech
• payments to MPs
• freedom from arrest
• composition of Parliament
• enforcement of breaches of privilege.

Key term: parliamentary privilege
Grants legal immunities to members of both Houses of Parliament so that they can perform their duties free from outside interference.

Freedom of speech

This is claimed in Article 9 of the Bill of Rights 1689: 'That the freedom of speech and debates or proceedings in Parliament ought not to be impeached or questioned in any court or place outside of Parliament'.

Absolute privilege

Debates and questions in Parliament are protected from any legal liability. This privilege, known as **absolute privilege**, extends to proceedings in the various committees of the House. Therefore, an MP is protected from being sued for defamation, prosecuted for breach of the Official Secrets Act and from contempt of court for disobeying a court order not to name a party in a case.

Key term: absolute privilege

What is said or written is not liable in defamation, even if the statement is untrue or malicious.

Absolute privilege applies when there is a close connection between the speech and parliamentary proceedings. Discussions between an MP and a minister concerning a parliamentary question would be an example. This principle was extended in *Makudi v Baron Triesman of Tottenham* [2014] EWCA Civ 179. Lord Triesman gave evidence to a Commons select committee and accused FIFA of corruption. The committee asked him to repeat the allegations to a Football Association (FA) inquiry, which he did. This repetition was protected by absolute privilege, because of the very strong public interest in investigating the allegations.

Absolute privilege does not apply if it is not a proceeding in Parliament, as can be seen in the examples in **Table 2.3**.

Table 2.3: When absolute privilege does not apply

Buchanan v Jennings [2005] 1 AC 115	If an MP repeats the same allegations *outside* Parliament, they are not protected.
Rivlin v Bilainkin [1953] 1 QB 485	A member of the public posted a defamatory letter in the Houses of Parliament.
Strauss and the London Electricity Board 1958	An MP passed a letter from a constituent to the relevant minister. The House of Commons ruled that this was not a proceeding in Parliament.

Qualified privilege

If an MP is sued for defamation, they might be able to claim **qualified privilege**, that what they said was in the public interest, meaning that they are protected from liability, unless the claimant can prove that they were motivated by 'malice'. Malice requires the claimant to prove that the defendant did not believe what they said or wrote was true or were reckless as to whether it was or not. This would usually be a perfectly adequate defence for the MP. It applied when:

- an MP passed on a letter from a constituent, complaining about a firm of solicitors, to the Lord Chancellor in *Beech v Freeson* [1972] 1 QB 14
- a constituent wrote a letter to his MP complaining about a police officer and a magistrate in *R v Rule* [1937] 2 KB 375.

Key term: qualified privilege

What is said or written is not liable in defamation, if there was a public interest in making the statement and the statement was not malicious.

Exam warning

Absolute privilege and qualified privilege *are not the same*. The latter only gives limited protection from defamation. For example, *Strauss MP* (see **Absolute privilege**) did not have absolute privilege, but he did have qualified privilege.

Publication of parliamentary proceedings

Parliament publishes an official record of its proceedings known as 'Hansard' as well as many other official papers. The courts did not consider that these publications had any legal protection from libel in *Stockdale v Hansard* (1839) 9 AD & E 1, so Parliament enacted the Parliamentary Papers Act 1840 awarding its official publications absolute privilege.

Newspapers and other media are protected by qualified privilege if they publish a fair and accurate report of the parliamentary proceedings. The report does not have to be word for word. It can be a selective summary provided that it appears fair and accurate to the reasonable reader and avoids gratuitous and irrelevant comments: *Curistan v Times Newspapers* [2007] EWHC 926.

Parliamentary proceedings in court

Article 9 of the Bill of Rights means that the courts cannot 'question' a proceeding in Parliament, hence the courts will not allow parliamentary proceedings to be used as evidence in libel cases. Nor will the courts investigate whether Parliament properly considered an EU directive when passing an Act: *R (HS2 Action Alliance Ltd) v Secretary of State for Transport* [2014] UKSC 3.

The courts, however, will look at a public document such as the Register of Members Interests and will consult the record of a parliamentary debate to help the court decide the meaning of a statute: *Pepper v Hart* [1992] 2 WLR 1032.

Revision tip

The law here is a little unclear, but what the courts are trying to avoid is criticising or commenting upon what Parliament has done.

Payments to MPs

Before 1911, MPs were not paid a salary, so they have always had other jobs. Even today, most MPs have outside employment, particularly consultancies. As Parliament is supreme, it makes its own rules to try to prevent MPs promoting outside interests for payment. It has passed numerous resolutions on this subject, which are now summarised in the MPs' code of conduct.

MPs' code of conduct

- MPs must disclose 'any relevant interest in any proceedings of the House or its committees, and in any communications with ministers, members, public officials or public office holder'.
- MPs must also enter all their financial interests including other jobs, company directorships, consultancies, donations, gifts and hospitality, trips abroad paid for by others, land, shareholdings and the employment of family members on parliamentary business, in the publicly available Register of Members' Interests.
- MPs' consultancy contracts must be entered upon the register in full.
- MPs may not have contracts, which restrict their independence in Parliament. Nor may the other party to the contract use it to seek to control the MP's conduct in Parliament.
- MPs are prohibited from 'lobbying', meaning that they may not promote a matter with an MP, minister, or public official for financial gain.

We can see how these strict rules work in **Practice example 2.4**.

Practice example 2.4

A wealthy businessman pays an MP money to ask a parliamentary question. Is this allowed?

Definitely not. Even if the MP registered and declared the payment, the independence of the MP is compromised. Both the MP and the businessman commit a contempt of Parliament and could be punished as explained in enforcement of breaches of privilege below.

The Parliamentary Commissioner for Standards
An independent Parliamentary Commissioner for Standards maintains the register and enforces these rules. Complaints about breach of these rules may be made by an MP or a member of the public to this commissioner. The commissioner can investigate, and less serious breaches are dealt with by the MP apologising and the register being corrected. More serious breaches are referred to the House of Commons Committee on Standards and Privileges.

MPs' expenses
MPs may claim various allowances and expenses, in addition to their salary. After a scandal in 2009 about MPs claiming excessive expenses, Parliament handed over its control of MPs' expenses and pay to the Independent Parliamentary Standards Authority (IPSA), created by the Parliamentary Standards Act 2009. IPSA employs a compliance officer who advises and enforces the rules.

Freedom from arrest
In the past, MPs could not be arrested while the House was sitting, but nowadays this privilege is only claimed for civil arrest, such as for non-payment of maintenance, which would seldom occur.

Composition of Parliament
Parliament claims the right to determine who is qualified to vote in elections and who is eligible to become an MP. Nowadays this is regulated in detail by the various Representation of the People Acts and the matter would be left to the courts to decide.

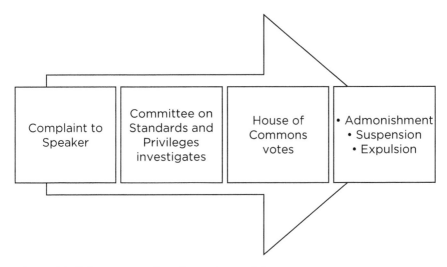

Figure 2.1: Enforcement of parliamentary privilege

Enforcement of breaches of privilege

Breaking the rules of parliamentary privilege is known as a contempt of Parliament and is dealt with by Parliament itself. The Speaker deals with minor offences, such as misbehaviour in the House by MPs and members of the public. He might ask the offender to leave Parliament for the day. The Speaker refers more serious matters to the Committee on Standards and Privileges to investigate and decide on any appropriate punishment. Whatever this committee decides must be approved by a vote of the full House of Commons. The penalties are admonishment (a reprimand), suspension without pay for a period of days and expulsion, where the member ceases to be an MP (**Figure 2.1**).

Under the Recall of MPs Act 2015, if an MP is suspended for 10 days or more, is convicted and receives a custodial sentence or is convicted of an offence relating to financial allowances, the Speaker must inform their constituency. If 10% of the electorate in that constituency request it in a petition, that MP is required to stand for re-election.

Making false expenses claims is also subject to the criminal law and parliamentary privilege does not prohibit prosecution: *R v Chaytor* [2010] UKSC 52. Have a look at **Practice example 2.5** for an illustration of this.

Practice example 2.5

After parliamentary debates have finished for the day two MPs adjourn to the House of Commons bar. After a few drinks, they quarrel and A hits B in the face. Would this be dealt with as a criminal offence?

Probably not. The Speaker would be able to deal with the matter and punish A for his misbehaviour. If A had committed a serious offence, Parliament would vote to waive its privilege, as in *R v Chaytor* above, and allow the police to prosecute.

Summary: parliamentary privilege

| WHAT is parliamentary privilege? | The right of Parliament to conduct its own affairs without outside interference. |
| HOW does this work? | The courts cannot investigate how Parliament works or say that Parliament is wrong. |

■ KEY POINT CHECKLIST

This chapter has covered the following key knowledge points. You can use these to structure your revision, making sure to recall the key details for each point, as covered in this chapter.

- The powers of Parliament.
- The functions of the House of Commons and the House of Lords.
- Parliamentary sovereignty.
- Parliamentary privilege and the protection of free speech.
- Parliamentary privilege and the control of MPs' financial interests.

■ KEY TERMS AND CONCEPTS

- parliamentary sovereignty (**page 26**)
- parliamentary privilege (**page 30**)
- absolute privilege (**page 31**)
- qualified privilege (**page 32**)

■ SQE1-STYLE QUESTIONS

QUESTION 1

A client approaches a solicitor about a parliamentary Bill that he opposes. The House of Commons has agreed to it twice, but the House of Lords has rejected it.

What steps could the client take to prevent the Bill becoming law?

A. The client could petition the monarch to refuse the royal assent. ⌒

B. The client could ask the Supreme Court to declare the Bill unconstitutional. ✗

C. The client could petition the House of Lords to reject the Bill again. ✗

D. The client could petition the monarch, but they would not refuse the royal assent. *(Don't ignore obvious correct*

E. The client could petition the House of Commons to reconsider. ✓

statements).

QUESTION 2

A campaigning group that protects the rights of children claims that a new Children's Act contravenes the United Nations Convention on the Rights of the Child. The UK is a party to this international treaty.

Which of the following is the most likely outcome for the group?

A. The group could apply to the European Court of Human Rights.

B. The group could apply to the International Court of Justice, which is the court of the United Nations. ⌒

C. The group could apply to a UK court, but that court would enforce the Children's Act.

D. The group could apply to a UK court and that court would hold the Children's Act invalid.

E. The group could apply to a UK court and that court would declare that the Children's Act was incompatible with human rights.

QUESTION 3

A client has had his land confiscated by an Act of Parliament. He claims that, contrary to Parliament's own standing orders, he was not notified that this was being considered, so he was unable to put forward his arguments that the Bill should not be passed.

Which of the following is the most likely decision of the court in this matter?

A. The court will investigate whether the client's claim was true.

B. The court will declare the Act to be invalid.

C. The court will interpret the Act so that it does not deprive the client of his right to property.

D. The court will judicially review the Act for breach of natural justice.

E. The court will not investigate the client's claim.

QUESTION 4

During a debate in the House of Commons, an MP accuses a famous businessman of a serious criminal offence. The MP is interviewed outside Parliament, where he repeats the allegation. A newspaper reports the debate and the interview with the MP. The businessman wants to sue for defamation.

Which of the following best summarises the legal position?

A. Only the MP can be sued.

B. Only the newspaper can be sued.

C. Neither the newspaper nor the MP can be sued.

D. The MP cannot be sued.

E. Both the MP and newspaper can be sued.

QUESTION 5

A client is an MP, who is employed as a parliamentary consultant, by the Road Transport Group, at an annual salary of £10,000. The Road Transport Group opposes proposed new restrictions on the hours worked by lorry drivers. The Group instructs their consultant MP to vote against these measures in Parliament and say that they will no longer employ him if he refuses.

Which of the following best summarises the position of the client?

A. An MP cannot have a job with an outside body.

B. An MP cannot receive any payments from an outside body.

C. An MP can be dismissed from their consultancy with an outside body.

D. An MP cannot be instructed on how to vote by an outside body.

E. An MP can have a job with an outside body.

■ ANSWERS TO QUESTIONS

Answers to 'What do you know already?' questions at the start of the chapter

1) False. The royal assent must also be given, and Acts passed under the Parliament Act 1949 are not agreed by the Lords.
2) The answer was (c). A Parliament cannot prevent a future Parliament from legislating in any way that it wants, otherwise that future Parliament would not be sovereign.
3) True. An Act may contain a special procedure, but that procedure can be ignored by a future Parliament.
4) The answer was (b). An Act of Parliament can do anything, including allowing EU law to have supremacy.
5) Yes. MPs have no immunity from the criminal law, although Parliament may claim the right to deal with criminal behaviour during or connected to parliamentary proceedings.
6) The answer was (c). Newspaper reports of parliamentary proceedings have qualified privilege if they are fair and accurate.

Answers to end-of-chapter SQE1-style questions

Question 1:
   The correct answer was D. This is because under the sovereignty of Parliament, the courts will not question an Act of Parliament nor investigate the procedure under which it was passed. This includes the Parliament Act procedures, where if a Bill is passed twice by the House of Commons, the agreement of the House of Lords is not required. The Bill will still require the royal assent, but this is never refused.
Question 2:
   The correct answer was C. This is because under the sovereignty of Parliament, the courts will not question an Act of Parliament. Whether the Act contravenes international law or not is irrelevant.
Question 3:
   The correct answer was E. This is because under the sovereignty of Parliament, the courts will not question an Act of Parliament nor investigate the procedure under which it was passed. There are many theoretical arguments that, in certain circumstances, an Act of Parliament would be invalid, but none of them have succeeded in court.

Question 4:

> The correct answer was A. What is said in a parliamentary proceeding, such as a debate, is protected by absolute privilege. If, however, it is repeated outside Parliament, there is no protection from defamation proceedings. Fair and accurate reports of parliamentary proceedings are protected by qualified privilege, but not the repetition of statements made outside of a parliamentary proceeding.

Question 5:

> The correct answer was D. MPs are permitted outside interests, although they must register them, but the body or person that employs them must not try to control the MP's conduct in Parliament. If the employer told their MP how to vote, this would be a breach of parliamentary privilege and they could be punished for contempt of Parliament.

■ KEY CASES, RULES, STATUTES AND INSTRUMENTS

The SQE1 Assessment Specification does not require you to remember the names of these cases, but the principles contained in them are important:

- *R (Jackson) v Attorney General* [2006] 1 AC 262 – the Parliament Acts allow an Act of Parliament to be passed, without the agreement of the House of Lords.
- *R (Miller) v Secretary of State for Exiting the EU* [2017] – an Act of the UK Parliament overrides the legislation of the devolved legislatures.
- *R v Secretary of State for Transport ex parte Factortame* [1991] 1 AC 603 – EU law had supremacy over a UK Act, until the UK withdrew from the EU.
- *R (HS2 Action Alliance Ltd) v Secretary of State for Transport* [2014] UKSC 3 – the courts will not question Parliament's procedures.

Central government and devolved institutions

■ MAKE SURE YOU KNOW

This chapter will cover the main aspects of central government and devolved institutions that you will need to know and be able to apply to scenarios, problems and situations for your SQE1 assessment.

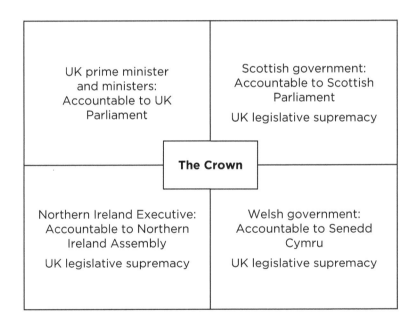

■ SQE ASSESSMENT ADVICE

As you work through this chapter, remember to pay particular attention in your revision to:
- the powers of the prime minister
- ministerial responsibility
- government accountability to Parliament
- the Scottish government and Scottish Parliament
- the Welsh government and Welsh Parliament
- the Northern Ireland Executive and Northern Ireland Assembly
- the sovereignty of the UK Parliament.

■ WHAT DO YOU KNOW ALREADY?

Have a go at these questions before reading this chapter. If you find some difficult or cannot remember the answers, make a note to look more closely at that subtopic during your revision.

1) How is the prime minister chosen?
   a) the monarch decides
   b) the electorate decides
   c) Parliament decides.
   [The prime minister, page 43]

2) The prime minister wants to appoint a prominent businessman, who is not a Member of Parliament (MP), as secretary of state for employment. Can the prime minister do this?
   [Ministers of the Crown, page 44]

3) What is the Ministerial Code?
   a) legal rules for government ministers
   b) advice for government ministers
   c) codified conventions for government ministers.
   [Ministerial responsibility, page 44]

4) Accountability means that the government must obtain permission from Parliament for everything that they do. True or false?
   [Accountability to Parliament, page 46]

5) Devolution means that the UK Parliament has shared its powers with the legislatures of Scotland, Wales, and Northern Ireland. True or false?
   [Devolved institutions, page 49]

6) How could Scotland, Wales or Northern Ireland leave the UK?
   a) with an Act from their own legislature
   b) with a UK Act of Parliament
   c) with an Act from the UK Parliament and their own legislature.
   [Devolved institutions, page 49]

CENTRAL GOVERNMENT AND ACCOUNTABILITY

The central government of the UK consists of the Crown, **government ministers** and the civil servants that work for them. The Parliament of the UK examines the work that they do and holds them to account. A knowledge of central government is required for SQE1, so in this section you can revise:

- the role of the prime minister
- the role of ministers of the Crown
- ministerial responsibility
- **accountability** to Parliament.

The prime minister

Legally, the head of state of the UK is the monarch, but by convention the **prime minister** exercises the powers of the monarch, known as the royal prerogative, in their name. The office of prime minister exists by convention too and most of his/her powers also only exist by convention (see **Chapter 1, page 13** for conventions).

Key term: prime minister
The prime minister is the head of the UK government and uses the legal powers of the monarch.

The prime minister is appointed by the monarch, and the convention is that he/she must be able to command the support of a majority of MPs in the House of Commons. Usually this means that the prime minister is the leader of the majority political party, but this is not always the case (eg if there is a coalition government). The powers of the prime minister include:

- appointment of ministers of the Crown
- appointment of the Cabinet
- structure of government departments
- control of armed forces
- control of intelligence and security services
- foreign affairs including international treaties
- official appointments (eg peerages and honours)
- management of the Civil Service – the prime minister is also minister for the Civil Service
- control of Cabinet meetings
- creation of Cabinet committees.

Ministers of the Crown

Government ministers are, by convention, chosen from among the MPs and Lords who support the majority party or parties in the Commons. Ministers form the government and oversee the various government departments, which are staffed by civil servants. The chief ministers form the Cabinet. This is a group of, usually, just over 20 ministers, which is the main coordinating and decision-making body of the government. The highest rank of minister, secretary of state, are all members of the Cabinet. They head government departments and are assisted by lower-ranking ministers, ministers of state and below that parliamentary under secretaries of state. There are about 100 of these other ministers and they too are drawn from the ranks of the majority party.

Key term: government minister
The men and women who run the government. They are chosen by the prime minister from among MPs and Lords.

Ministerial responsibility

The behaviour of ministers is governed by convention and many of these conventions have been written down in the 'Ministerial Code', but not enacted into law. The prime minister enforces the code and, if a minister breaks the code, the prime minister might require their resignation. Ministers have control over those that work for them. The minister takes the credit or blame for their own behaviour and the performance of their department. We can see some examples from the Ministerial Code in **Table 3.1**.

Table 3.1: The Ministerial Code

Confidentiality	Opinions expressed in the Cabinet and its committees are private. Ministers must not disclose them. This is a convention and not enforceable in law: *Attorney General v Jonathan Cape* [1976] QB 752
Freedom of Information Act 2000	Cabinet proceedings and communications with ministers can be disclosed, if the court thinks it is in the public interest. A secretary of state may overrule the court decision, but only if the courts are satisfied that they have reasonable grounds: *R (Evans) v Attorney General* [2015] UKSC 21.

The Ministerial Code (continued)

Being truthful, especially to Parliament, is of paramount importance	Information must be accurate and truthful, and errors must be corrected as soon as possible. Ministers who knowingly mislead Parliament will be expected to offer their resignation.
Ministers must ensure that no conflict arises, or appears to arise, between their public duties and their private interests	Examples include accepting gifts or hospitality or using their ministerial post to advance their private business interests.
Ministers must behave with honesty and integrity	Examples include scandals in their private life, perhaps of a sexual nature, or financial misconduct or criminal convictions unconnected to their official role.

Have a look at **Practice example 3.1** for how ministerial responsibility works.

Practice example 3.1

John Profumo was the secretary of state for war and was married. He had a sexual relationship with Christine Keeler, who also had a sexual relationship with a Russian diplomat. Profumo denied this to fellow ministers, the prime minister and to the House of Commons. He resigned in 1962. Which part of the Ministerial Code had he broken?

Perhaps there was a conflict between his public duty and his private interests, but the clear breach was the lie to the House of Commons. Ministers must retain the confidence of the House.

Political neutrality of civil servants

The employment of civil servants is controlled by the Constitutional Reform and Governance Act 2010. Although this Act states they are managed by the minister for the Civil Service (prime minister), their employment is controlled by an independent body, the Civil Service Commission. Civil servants must be politically impartial and serve the current government.

Ministerial responsibility for civil servants

Civil servants often carry out work about which the minister might know little. The Ministerial Code states that 'ministers have a duty to Parliament to account, and be held to account, for the policies, decisions and actions of their departments and agencies'. This comes from the

Chrichel Down guidelines issued by the Home Secretary in 1954. A minister must take the blame and explain to Parliament even if a civil servant has not followed orders. In rare cases, if Parliament strongly disapproves, the minister might be expected to resign. The minister for agriculture, Sir Thomas Dugdale, resigned over Chrichel Down.

> **Exam warning**
>
> Ministerial responsibility is governed by conventions. These are not as clear cut as laws and no court rules on whether a convention has been broken. Therefore, there can be differences of opinion about what conventions require. SQE1 only asks you to give the most likely out of five possible answers, so do not worry if none of the five seem completely correct, just go for the best of the five.

Ministers are legally liable

Ministers are legally responsible for what their civil servants do. The minister is sued, not the civil servant: *Carltona v Commissioner of Works* [1943] 2 All ER 560.

Ministers of the Crown have no immunity from the law. Injunctions may be issued against them and if they disobey, they are in contempt of court: *M v Home Office* [1994] 1 AC 377.

Accountability to Parliament

A government needs to maintain the support of a majority of MPs in the House of Commons to pass the Acts of Parliament that it requires. The government must explain what it is doing to Parliament to maintain its support. MPs and Lords will criticise, ask questions and investigate what the government is doing. According to the Ministerial Code, 'ministers should be as open as possible with Parliament and the public, refusing to provide information only when disclosure would not be in the public interest'. There are parliamentary procedures that enable MPs to scrutinise the activities of the government, which we will see in what follows.

> **Key term: accountability**
>
> The government is required to justify its decisions and actions.

Parliamentary Bills

The House of Commons and House of Lords must vote to approve a Bill before it becomes an Act. There are opportunities to debate the Bill and examine it in detail during the committee stage (see **Chapter 5, page 79**).

Questions

Ministers from all the government departments and the prime minister must appear before the House of Commons and answer questions. Prime Minister's Question Time takes place every Wednesday. Ministers only answer on their area of responsibility, but the prime minister is responsible for the whole of the government. Questions can raise grievances, reveal mistakes and obtain information. MPs may also submit written questions.

Debates

MPs have opportunities to initiate a debate, using daily adjournment debates and early day motions, on a subject of their choosing. Twenty days are allocated for opposition-day debates (formerly called supply days), where the opposition may choose the main subject of parliamentary business.

Select committees

These are committees of backbench MPs who scrutinise the work of the government. Their membership is in proportion to party strength in the Commons, which does mean that the government has a majority. The members of each committee elect their own chair. Many of the committees have an opposition chair, including the powerful Public Accounts Committee. It checks whether the government is spending public money properly on the purposes approved by Parliament.

Each government department has a select committee of 11 MPs examining the work of that department and reporting to Parliament (eg the Select Committee on Health and Social Care). These committees have the following powers:

- The power to choose which part of their department's work they want to investigate and report to the full House of Commons.
- The power to send for persons, papers and records and to appoint specialist advisers.
- The full House of Commons can compel a minister, civil servant, MP or member of the public to attend.
- The Ministerial Code states that ministers should require their civil servants to be as helpful and truthful as possible.
- Members of the public who refuse to attend can be punished by the House of Commons for contempt of Parliament, but this would only be a reprimand.

Have a look at **Practice example 3.2** for an illustration of the powers of a select committee.

Practice example 3.2

The government has proposed a parliamentary Bill that will require patients to pay a fee to consult their doctor. An MP is opposed to this and is also chair of the departmental select committee on health. Can the MP use this committee to stop this Bill becoming law?

No. Departmental committees do not have to approve Bills. The committee could choose to investigate the new payments and might criticise, but it is up to the majority in Parliament whether the Bill becomes law or not. See Figure 3.1 for the parliamentary procedures to hold ministers to account.

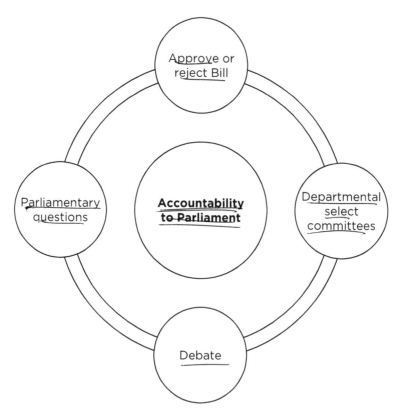

Figure 3.1: Parliamentary procedures to hold ministers to account

Summary: central government and accountability

WHAT is the UK central government?	The King, the prime minister, ministers of the Crown and the Civil Service.
WHAT is accountability?	The central government must explain and justify what it does to Parliament.
WHY?	So that the government is controlled by MPs on behalf of the electorate.

DEVOLVED INSTITUTIONS

SQE1 requires you to know about devolved institutions. Scotland, Wales and Northern Ireland were once separate countries and desired more powers of self-government. Hence, the Parliament of the UK delegated powers of government and legislation in the Scotland Act 1998, the Government of Wales Act 1998 and the Northern Ireland Act 1998. Those Acts have since been amended, increasing the powers of those countries. In this section you can revise:

• Scotland
• Wales
• Northern Ireland
• European Union (EU) withdrawal and **devolution**.

Key term: devolution

The UK Parliament has delegated some of its power. It has not been permanently transferred and can be recovered.

Scotland

Scotland had its own Parliament until Union with England in 1707 and so it has the most powerful devolved government.

The Scottish Parliament

There are 129 members of the Scottish Parliament. A total of 73 are elected for their constituency under the first-past-the-post system and 56 additional members are elected for regions under the party list system of proportional representation. General elections are held every five years, unless two-thirds of the Parliament vote for an earlier election.

The Scottish government

The Scottish government comprises a first minister, who would usually be whoever has a majority in the Parliament, and other ministers appointed by the first minister. Section 1 of the Scotland Act 2016 lays down that the 'Scottish Parliament and the Scottish government are a permanent part of the UK's constitutional arrangements' and that they can only be abolished if the people of Scotland vote for it in a referendum.

> **Revision tip**
>
> Although s 1 of the Scotland Act 2016 says that these arrangements are permanent, remember that the UK Parliament is sovereign and could repeal this section if it wanted.

Legislative competence

The Scotland Act 1998 makes clear that the UK Parliament retains its sovereign power to legislate for Scotland. The Scottish Parliament has limited powers to legislate. It cannot make laws on:

- matters outside of Scotland, nor any laws contrary to the European Convention on Human Rights (ECHR)
- the Scotland Act itself, the Human Rights Act 1998, the European Communities Act 1972, the EU (Withdrawal) Act 2018
- 'reserved matters', namely the constitution, which includes the Crown, the Union of England and Scotland, the UK Parliament, the highest Scottish courts, the registration of political parties, foreign affairs, Civil Service, defence and treason; there are also detailed reservations for financial and economic matters, home affairs, trade and industry, energy, transport, social security, regulation of the professions, employment, health and media and culture.

The Scottish Parliament does, however, have the right to set its own rates of income tax. If an Act of the Scottish Parliament is not within its **legislative competence** it is not law, and a court may suspend the effect of the Act until the defect is corrected. You can read about some cases illustrating the legislative competence of the Scottish Parliament in **Table 3.2**.

> **Key term: legislative competence**
>
> Unlike the sovereign UK Parliament, which has unlimited power to make laws, the legislatures of Scotland, Wales and Northern Ireland only have power to make laws on the subjects specified by the UK Parliament.

Scottish independence

Under s 30 of the Scotland Act 1998, a UK Order in Council may grant the Scottish Parliament the right to legislate on a reserved matter.

Table 3.2: Cases illustrating the legislative competence of the Scottish Parliament

Axa General Assurance v Lord Advocate [2011] UKSC 46	A Scottish Act of Parliament did not infringe the ECHR. The court would respect the decision of the elected body.
Salvesen v Riddell [2013] UKSC 22	The Scottish Act was incompatible with the ECHR as it infringed the right to property. The Scottish Parliament and ministers must find a solution.
Christian Institute v Lord Advocate [2016] UKSC 51	The Scottish Act was incompatible with Article 8 of the ECHR, the right to a private life.
Imperial Tobacco v Lord Advocate [2012] SC 297	A Scottish Act, which restricted tobacco advertising, was for the protection of health, upon which the Scottish Parliament could legislate, not consumer protection, which was a reserved matter.

This was done to enable the Scottish Parliament to pass the Scottish Independence Referendum Act 2013, which allowed that referendum to be held in 2014. The 'constitution' is a reserved matter. Have a look at **Practice example 3.3** for an illustration of this.

Practice example 3.3

The Scottish Parliament and its first minister want to pass an Act allowing a referendum to be held on independence from the UK. Can the Scottish Parliament do this?

The Scottish Parliament is not permitted to legislate on the constitution or the Union with England. However, if the referendum was held merely to gauge public opinion on this issue it might be legal. Legal opinion in 2013 was that the Scottish Parliament did not have the power to hold a referendum, but this has never been tested in court.

Wales

In 1998, Wales was allowed to enact secondary but not primary legislation. Since then its powers of self-government have been increased and it can now pass Acts of the Welsh Parliament (Senedd Cymru).

The Welsh Parliament

There are 60 members of the Senedd Cymru, formerly known as the Welsh Assembly. A total of 40 are elected for their constituency under the first-past-the-post system and 20 additional members are elected for the region under the party list system of proportional representation. General elections are held every five years, unless two-thirds of the Parliament vote for an earlier election.

The Welsh government

The Welsh government comprises a first minister, who would usually be whoever has a majority in the Parliament, and 12 other ministers appointed by the first minister. Section 1 of the Wales Act 2017 lays down that the 'Welsh Parliament and the Welsh government are a permanent part of the UK's constitutional arrangements' and that they can only be abolished if the people of Wales vote for it in a referendum.

Legislative competence

The Government of Wales Act 2006 makes clear that the UK Parliament retains its sovereign power to legislate for Wales. The Senedd has limited powers to legislate. It cannot make laws on:

- matters outside of Wales, nor any laws contrary to the ECHR
- the Government of Wales Act itself, the Human Rights Act 1998, the European Communities Act 1972, the EU (Withdrawal) Act 2018
- 'reserved matters', namely the constitution, which includes the Crown, the union of Wales and England, the Parliament of the UK, the Civil Service, the registration of political parties, the courts and legal system, foreign affairs and defence; there are also more detailed reservations for financial and economic matters, home affairs, trade and industry, energy, transport, social security, regulation of the professions, employment, health and media and culture.

In contrast to Scotland, which has its own separate law and legal system, Wales has the same legal system as England, which is why the Senedd has no power to legislate in this area. If an Act of the Senedd is not within its legislative competence it is not law, and a court may suspend the effect of the Act until the defect is corrected. The courts have liberally interpreted the powers of the Senedd as we can see in *Agricultural Sector (Wales) Bill – Attorney General's Reference* [2014] UKSC 43. An Act of the Welsh Assembly regulated agricultural wages. This fell under agriculture, which was devolved, not employment, which was reserved and so was within the legislative competence of the assembly.

Northern Ireland

A key issue for Northern Ireland is whether its people want to remain part of the UK or leave and join with the Republic of Ireland. Unionist political parties wish to remain in the UK, but nationalist parties wish to merge with the Republic. Section 1 of the Northern Ireland Act guarantees that this will be decided by a referendum. Have a look at **Practice example 3.4** for an illustration of this.

Practice example 3.4

Nationalist parties win a majority in a general election and wish to leave the UK. The Northern Ireland Assembly passes an Act without holding a referendum, stating that Northern Ireland has left the UK and joined the Republic of Ireland. What would be the effect of this Act?

It would not be law. The assembly has no power to legislate to change a UK Act of Parliament. Only the UK Parliament can repeal or amend the Northern Ireland Act 1998.

The Northern Ireland Assembly

There are 90 members of the Northern Ireland Assembly. There are 18 constituencies, each of which elect five members under the single transferable vote system. Elections are held every five years but may be held earlier if a two-thirds majority agree. Legislation is normally passed by a simple majority, but some measures may only be passed if they have 'cross-community support'. A majority of both nationalist and unionist members must vote for it.

The Northern Ireland Executive

There must be both a first minister and a deputy first minister, the first minister coming from the largest political party of the largest political designation (unionist) and the deputy from the largest political party of the second largest political designation (nationalist). The first minister and deputy first minister are required to act jointly. The assembly appoints the 10 other ministers, in proportion to the party strength in that body. These ministers form the executive with the first ministers.

Legislative competence

The Northern Ireland Act 1998 makes clear that the UK Parliament retains its sovereign power to legislate for Northern Ireland. The devolution scheme is different to Scotland and Wales and the Northern

Ireland Assembly has more limited legislative powers. It cannot make laws on:

* matters outside of Northern Ireland, nor any laws contrary to the ECHR or any laws that discriminate on the basis of religious belief or political opinion
* Human Rights Act 1998, the European Communities Act 1972, the EU (Withdrawal) Act 2018
* 'excepted matters' that cannot be transferred to the assembly, including the Crown, the UK Parliament, international relations, defence, tax, immigration, honours, treason and national security
* 'reserved' matters that might one day be transferred by the UK government, for example financial services, pensions regulation, international trade, financial markets and services, competition law, consumer safety, telecommunications, data protection, intellectual property and criminal law relating to terrorism.

Exam warning

Be careful here: the powers of the three devolved legislatures are not identical. What they have in common though is that they cannot legislate on certain matters and cannot contradict the UK Parliament.

EU withdrawal and devolution

Although the devolved legislatures have no power over international relations or relations with the EU, leaving affects some of the matters devolved to them.

Legislative consent motions (the Sewel Convention)

Section 2 of the Scotland Act 2016 and the Wales Act 2016 states that 'it is recognised that the Parliament of the UK will not normally legislate with regard to devolved matters without the consent of the Scottish (Welsh) Parliament'. If the UK Parliament proposes legislation on a devolved matter, the Scottish Parliament or Welsh Parliament draws up a Legislative Consent Motion to indicate whether it agrees or not. However, even if the Scottish or Welsh Parliament refuse consent, as the UK Parliament has supremacy, the UK Act upon a devolved matter would still be valid.

The UK Parliament is sovereign

In *R (Miller) v Secretary of State for Exiting the European Union* [2017] UKSC 5 the Supreme Court ruled that s 2 merely recognised the existence of a constitutional convention known as the Sewel Convention, which could not be enforced as a law. Even though leaving the EU would affect the devolved powers of the Scottish Parliament, Senedd Cymru and the Northern Ireland Assembly, the devolved legislatures did not have a legal veto on withdrawal. The Parliament of the UK was sovereign on this issue.

Summary: devolved institutions	
WHAT are the devolved institutions?	The governments and legislatures of Scotland, Wales and Northern Ireland.
WHAT do they do?	They have government and legislative power for their country.
WHO is in control?	The UK Parliament, which grants these powers and can remove them.

■ KEY POINT CHECKLIST

This chapter has covered the following key knowledge points. You can use these to structure your revision, making sure to recall the key details for each point, as covered in this chapter.

- *Prime minister*: The monarch is the legal head of state, but by convention the prime minister acts in her name and uses her legal powers.
- *Government minister*: They run the government. They are chosen by the prime minister from among MPs and Lords.
- *Ministerial responsibility*: Ministers bear the political and legal responsibility for what they themselves and the civil servants working for them do.
- *Accountability to Parliament*: The prime minister and his/her ministers must explain and justify what they do to Parliament.
- *Devolved institutions*: Scotland, Wales and Northern Ireland have their own governments and legislatures. They only have the power to legislate granted by the UK Parliament. The UK Parliament can take that power back.

■ KEY TERMS AND CONCEPTS

- prime minister (**page 43**)
- government minister (**page 44**)
- accountability (**page 46**)
- devolution (**page 49**)
- legislative competence (**page 50**)

■ SQE1-STYLE QUESTIONS

QUESTION 1

The prime minister wishes to appoint a key adviser as a Cabinet minister. The appointment of ministers is governed by convention.

Which of the following conventions would govern this appointment?

A. The adviser must be a member of the House of Commons or the House of Lords.

B. The adviser must be a member of the House of Commons. ×

C. The adviser must be nominated by the Cabinet. ✓

D. The adviser must be nominated by the prime minister's political party. ✗

E. The adviser must be a member of the House of Lords. ×

QUESTION 2

A civil servant in the Home Office authorises the unlawful deportation of an alleged illegal immigrant.

Which of the following is the most appropriate person against whom legal action should be taken?

A. The civil servant. ✗

B. Her Majesty's government. ✓

C. The secretary of state for home affairs. .

D. The attorney general. ×

E. The prime minister. ✗

QUESTION 3

A government minister has been convicted for driving while disqualified. The prime minister seeks advice upon whether he must require the minister to resign. A solicitor consults the Ministerial Code to advise the prime minister.

Which of the following best describes the position under the code?

A. The minister must resign if he commits a criminal offence.

B. The minister must resign if he is in breach of collective responsibility.

C. The minister must resign if he is in breach of Cabinet confidentiality.

D. The minister must resign if he compromises the political impartiality of the Civil Service.

E. The minister must resign if he knowingly misleads Parliament.

QUESTION 4

The first minister of Northern Ireland wishes to appoint a member of his political party, John, as a minister.

Which of the following best describes the procedure for doing this?

A. The first minister nominates John and the monarch appoints him.
    wales, uk, scotland.

B. The first minister appoints John.

C. The first minister appoints John with the agreement of the deputy first minister.

D. A political party in the Northern Ireland Assembly nominates John.

E. The first minister appoints John with the agreement of the secretary of state for Northern Ireland.

QUESTION 5

An Act of the Scottish Parliament is passed, with a simple majority, declaring that Scotland is an independent country and no longer part of the UK.

Which of the following best describes the effect of this Act?

A. The Act would only be law in Scotland.

B. The Act would not be law because it is outside the legislative competence of the Scottish Parliament.

C. The Act would not be law because a two-thirds majority of the Scottish Parliament is required.

D. The Act would be law if the Supreme Court agreed.

E. The Act would be law for all of the UK.

■ ANSWERS TO QUESTIONS

Answers to 'What do you know already?' questions at the start of the chapter

1) The correct answer was (c). Whoever has a majority in Parliament becomes prime minister. The King legally makes the appointment, but by convention does not make a personal choice.
2) Legally yes, but by convention no. The secretary of state must be a member of the House of Commons or the House of Lords so that he can be accountable.
3) The correct answer was (c). The Ministerial Code summarises the accepted conventions, but it has never been made law by an Act of Parliament.
4) False. Sharing suggests that the UK Parliament and devolved legislatures are equal, but the UK Parliament remains sovereign and decides which powers to devolve and which powers to reclaim.
5) The correct answer was (b). As the UK Parliament is sovereign, only it can grant independence.

Answers to end-of-chapter SQE1-style questions

Question 1:
   The correct answer was A. This is because convention requires a minister to be a member of either of the two Houses of Parliament. Otherwise, the minster cannot be accountable to Parliament.

Question 2:
   The correct answer was C. This is because the government minister in charge of the department takes legal responsibility for what happens in their department.

Question 3:
   The correct answer was E. This is because the Ministerial Code tells ministers what they can and cannot do, but only in this example does it require resignation. Usually, resignation is left to the discretion of the prime minister.

Question 4:
   The correct answer was D. This is what the devolution legislation for Northern Ireland requires. It is unusual because in the government of the UK, Scotland and Wales the prime minister nominates a minister and the King appoints them.

Question 5:

The correct answer was B. This is because the devolution legislation for Scotland does not allow the Scottish Parliament to legislate on the Union with England or the constitution. Remember that the devolved legislatures have limited powers.

■ KEY CASES, RULES, STATUTES AND INSTRUMENTS

The SQE1 Assessment Specification does not require you to remember case names, but these cases contain important principles, which are worth remembering:

- *Attorney General v Jonathan Cape* [1976] QB 752 – conventions are not legally enforceable.
- *Carltona v Commissioner of Works* [1943] 2 All ER 560 – ministers are legally responsible for their civil servants.
- *R (Miller) v Secretary of State for Exiting the European Union* [2017] UKSC 5 – the UK Parliament is sovereign.

Prime Minister nominates a minister & King appoints them.

4

The Crown and the royal prerogative

■ MAKE SURE YOU KNOW

This chapter will cover the main aspects of the Crown and the royal prerogative that you will need to know and be able to apply to scenarios, problems and situations for your SQE1 assessment.

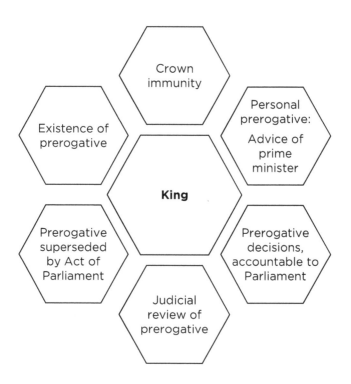

■ SQE ASSESSMENT ADVICE

The SQE1 Assessment Specification for constitutional and administrative law states that you must know about the 'core institutions of the state and how they interrelate'. This includes 'the monarch and the Crown' and 'prerogative power: relationship with legislation and constitutional conventions'.

As you work through this chapter, remember to pay particular attention in your revision to the following:
- the King is the legal head of state, but by convention his government acts in his name
- the Crown Proceedings Act 1947
- the King retains many legal powers, called the royal prerogative, which the government may use
- the courts may have to decide which prerogatives still exist
- the courts only judicially review some prerogatives
- the government is accountable to Parliament for its use of the prerogative.

■ WHAT DO YOU KNOW ALREADY?

Have a go at these questions before reading this chapter. If you find some difficult or cannot remember the answers, make a note to look more closely at that subtopic during your revision.

1) What legal powers does the King retain?
    [The whole chapter]
2) It is not possible to sue the Crown. True or false?
    [Crown proceedings, page 63]
3) All prerogative powers are now contained in Acts of Parliament. True or false?
    [The royal prerogative and Acts of Parliament, page 66]
4) Which of the following prerogative powers can be judicially reviewed?
    a) the refusal of a passport
    b) the ratification of a treaty
    c) the invasion of a foreign country.
    [Judicial review of the royal prerogative, page 68]
5) The government never needs the authorisation of Parliament to use its prerogative powers. True or false?
    [Accountability to Parliament for the prerogative, page 71]

THE CROWN

The word 'Crown' has two distinct meanings in constitutional law. It could mean the monarch, King Charles III or it could mean His Majesty's government, which includes government ministers, the Civil Service, the armed forces and land and other property belonging to the government. This section will help you revise:

• the role of the King
• Crown proceedings.

The role of the King

In the past, the King or Queen was the absolute ruler, but this is no longer the case. The term '**royal prerogative**' refers to the legal powers of the Crown that have survived.

Key term: royal prerogative

Constitutional theorist Albert Dicey's definition is: 'The residue of discretionary or arbitrary authority which at any given time is legally left in the hands of the Crown'. This means the remaining powers and privileges of the Crown.

The role of the King

The King is the head of state of the UK and its various overseas territories. In this role he performs symbolic and ceremonial functions. He is also head of state of 14 other, independent countries, the largest of which are Australia, Canada and New Zealand. Each of the 14 countries has its own governor general, who performs his role. The King is also head of the Commonwealth, an international organisation of countries, most of which were once ruled by the UK.

The personal prerogatives

Some of the prerogative powers are referred to as personal prerogatives, meaning that the King is still involved in their use. Here are some examples of personal prerogatives:

• Legally the King appoints the prime minister, but by convention this is always the person who commands a majority in the House of Commons. If no person could do this it would be left to the political parties to negotiate a coalition or a minority government. If the parties failed to agree upon a new prime minister and the national interest required it, the King could nominate his choice of prime minister, although this is most unlikely to happen.
• The prime minister decides who is to become a government minister and they are formally appointed by the King.

- Legally, the King decides when Parliament is summoned, when it is prorogued (not in session) and used to decide when it was dissolved (a general election is called). By convention the prime minister decided all these matters, but under the Fixed-Term Parliaments Act 2011, general elections are now every five years, unless the House of Commons decides by a two-thirds majority that there will be an earlier election or the government loses a vote of confidence and no other government can be found.
- A Bill from Parliament must receive the royal assent before it becomes an Act of Parliament. By convention, the King would not refuse his agreement to an Act.
- The grant of honours. The King accepts nominations from the government.

The King may advise the government

The convention is that His Majesty's government, that is government ministers, decide upon the use of the King's surviving legal prerogative powers. But it is equally the convention that the King must be consulted about these decisions. The nineteenth-century constitutional writer, Bagehot, said that the King or Queen had the right to advise, encourage or warn the prime minister or minister making the decision. That is still true today, meaning that the King or Queen can express an opinion, favourable or unfavourable, but the minister decides.

Crown proceedings

The King himself can do no wrong legally. He is not liable in criminal or civil law and cannot be arrested. This immunity does not extend to any other members of his family.

The Crown, meaning the government, used to have some immunities from the law, but these were restricted by the Crown Proceedings Act 1947:
- Under the Act the Crown retained its immunity from the criminal law.
- Under s 1, the Crown can be sued in contract.
- Under s 2, the Crown has liability in tort and has vicarious liability for its servants and agents.

Enforcement against the Crown

Section 21(1) states that court orders such as injunctions and specific performance could not be awarded against the Crown.
- In *M v Home Office* [1994] 1 AC 377, the Crown was interpreted to mean the Queen personally. Court orders could be made against

government ministers, and if they disobeyed they could be punished for contempt of court.

- In *R v Secretary of State for Transport ex parte Factortame (No 2)* [1991] AC 603, an interim injunction could be issued against the secretary of state. Have a look at **Practice example 4.1** for how this works.
- Under the Act, members of the armed forces could not sue for injuries sustained while on duty or on military premises, but this immunity was suspended by the armed forces (Crown Proceedings) Act 1987. It can be revived in times of war or national emergency.
- Under s 40(2) of the Crown Proceedings Act 1947, the Crown is not bound by an Act of Parliament unless it is expressly stated in the Act or it must be implied from the wording of the Act. In *Lord Advocate v Dumbarton DC* [1990] 1 All ER 1, the Crown was not bound by planning Acts of Parliament. Many modern Acts of Parliament expressly state that they apply to the Crown (eg the Human Rights Act 1998).
- Act of State is an ancient prerogative power, which holds that UK government actions taken against foreign citizens *outside* the UK are not actionable. This was not changed by the Crown Proceedings Act 1947.

Practice example 4.1

The Home Office is about to deport a person whom they believe to be an illegal immigrant. Can their lawyers prevent the Home Office from doing this?

This is what happened in *M v Home Office* [1994] 1 AC 377. If the claimant has a legal argument that they should be allowed to stay in the UK, the court can go further than just giving a judgment that this would be illegal. The court may issue an injunction ordering the Home Office not to deport, which the Home Office must obey.

Summary: the Crown

WHAT is the Crown?	It is either the King personally or His Majesty's government.
WHAT does the Crown do?	The King has many legal powers, which are used by the government, after consultation with him.
DOES the Crown have any legal privileges?	The King cannot be sued, but the government can.

THE ROYAL PREROGATIVE: REMAINING POWERS

Although it is still called the royal prerogative, these powers are now used by the government, rather than the King. They are executive powers, in that, legally, the government does not need the permission of Parliament to use them. It is even possible for the government to make prerogative laws, known as Orders in Council, without the agreement of Parliament. This section will help you revise:

• which prerogatives still exist
• the extent of a prerogative power.

The government and House of Commons both admit that it is not possible to compile a definitive list of prerogative power, but the following categories are generally accepted:

• *Government and Civil Service*. The government has control over the Civil Service and can establish new organisations (eg the BBC was created by a royal charter).
• *Justice system, mercy and pardon*. The power to keep the peace of the realm. Appointment of King's Counsel.
• *National security*. The intelligence and security services.
• *Foreign affairs*. Relations with other states. Signing and ratifying international treaties.
• *Defence of the realm*. Control of the armed forces. Deployment of troops.

Which prerogatives still exist?

Sometimes the existence of a prerogative power is disputed and then a court would have to decide whether the power ever existed and whether it still exists. In *BBC v Johns* [1965] Ch 32, the BBC claimed that, as part of the Crown, they were exempt from tax, but the court found no historical precedent for this. The government has always had the power to requisition or even destroy property in wartime, but it was not until the twentieth century that the courts recognised that compensation should be paid: *Attorney General v De Keyser's Royal Hotel* [1920] AC 508. As late as 1987, the courts accepted that the government had always had a prerogative power to keep the peace of the realm: *R v Secretary of State for the Home Department, ex parte Northumbria Police* [1987] 2 WLR 998.

The extent of the prerogative power

Identifying the precise extent of a prerogative power can enable a court to restrain abuse of government power for example, in *R (Miller) v The Prime Minister* [2019] UKSC 41.

The King or Queen has a prerogative power to prorogue (end) the current session of Parliament, although the convention is that the prime minister decides and the King or Queen orders it. Prime Minister Johnson decided upon a prorogation of 34 days, while Parliament was discussing withdrawal from the European Union (EU). The Supreme Court concluded that there was no legal prerogative power to suspend Parliament for such a long period. Parliament was sovereign and must be allowed to legislate and hold the government to account. The executive (prime minister and ministers) could not prevent this.

Exam warning

It is difficult to list all the prerogative powers that exist and even harder to remember them all. You can, however, usually work out whether a question is about a prerogative power. If it concerns the King or the prime minister, it means that you are looking at a prerogative power.

Summary: the royal prerogative: remaining powers

WHAT is the royal prerogative?	The remaining legal powers of the King.
WHO decides which powers remain?	The courts.
WHO is it used by? -	The government acting in the name of the King.

THE ROYAL PREROGATIVE AND ACTS OF PARLIAMENT

Over the centuries many prerogatives have been removed by Acts of Parliament, for example the Bill of Rights 1689. Many powers that were once prerogative powers have also been put on a statutory basis, such as the Security Service Act 1989, and the Civil Service was regulated by the Constitutional Reform and Governance Act 1989. This section will help you revise:
• statute and prerogative
• treaties and statute.

Statute and prerogative

If the government has the same power under the prerogative and statute, the government must use the statutory power.
• For example, in *Attorney General G v De Keyser's Royal Hotel* [1920] AC 508, it was decided that the government must compensate De

Keyser under the Defence of the Realm Act 1914. The sovereignty of Parliament must be respected, and this gave better protection to the citizen.

- In *R v Secretary of State for the Home Department, ex parte Fire Brigades Union* [1995] 2 AC 513, the Criminal Injuries Compensation Scheme was created by the royal prerogative. It had been replaced by the Criminal Justice Act 1988, but the secretary of state had never brought that Act into force. Instead, he was proposing to introduce a new prerogative scheme with reduced rates of compensation.
  - The House of Lords ruled that the executive could not use the prerogative to frustrate the will of Parliament. It was for Parliament, not the executive to repeal legislation.

Both cases made clear that, if the Acts of Parliament were repealed, then the prerogative power would revive and the government could use it.

Prerogative powers may exist in addition to statutory powers

More commonly the government has a mixture of statutory and prerogative powers. For example, UK citizenship is determined by statutory rules, but the issue of a passport, which authorises travel, is a prerogative power and at the discretion of the government. This mixture of powers can be seen in *R (G) v Home Secretary* [2013] 2 WLR 1277. G was deprived of his UK citizenship using the statutory power in the British Nationality Act 1981. As he was now an alien, the home secretary could use her prerogative power to deny him entry to the UK.

Treaties and statute

Becoming a party to a treaty is a prerogative power, so the government does not need Parliament's permission to join or leave a treaty, although Parliament is given the opportunity to comment on draft treaties. If, however, a treaty alters the law within the UK, an Act of Parliament is required. In *R (Miller) v Secretary of State for Exiting the European Union* [2017] UKSC 5, the government argued that they could use the royal prerogative to withdraw from the various EU treaties, but the Supreme Court said that this was illegal. The European Communities Act 1972 altered UK law and gave rights to UK citizens. Withdrawal would change this and that required an Act of Parliament.

Summary: the royal prerogative and Acts of Parliament	
WHAT is the effect of Acts of Parliament?	They supersede prerogative powers.
WHEN is the prerogative used?	The government use the prerogative when it does not have a statutory power.
WHEN is an Act of Parliament required?	To implement a treaty into UK law.

JUDICIAL REVIEW OF THE ROYAL PREROGATIVE

This section will enable you to revise when the courts will allow **judicial review** of the prerogative and when they will not. It was once thought that it was not possible to challenge prerogative acts using the process of judicial review.

Key term: judicial review

The process by which the courts control the exercise of government power. The courts decide whether the government has the legal power to do what it has done.

This was changed in: *R v Secretary of State for the Foreign and Commonwealth Office, ex parte The Council of Civil Service Unions* [1985] AC 374. The foreign secretary wanted to ban trade union membership for civil servants working at Government Communications, because he believed that this was a threat to national security. This was done by an Order in Council (legislation made under the prerogative). The unions argued that they had not been consulted, but the court said that they could not question the foreign secretary's decision on national security. The House of Lords said that it was possible to review other prerogative acts, but differed on when this was possible:

- Only some prerogatives could be reviewed. Lord Roskill gave a list of unreviewable areas, which were treaties, defence, mercy, honours, dissolution of Parliament and appointment of ministers. Subsequent cases have not followed this list.
- If the prerogative act affected the rights of citizens, it could be reviewed.

In summary, areas of high government policy were **non-justiciable**, but more everyday matters affecting citizens might be considered.

Table 4.1: The main bases of judicial review

Illegality	The government does not have the power to this.
Irrationality	No reasonable person would make that decision based on those facts.
Procedural impropriety	The correct procedure has not been followed, there has been a lack of consultation or there has not been a fair hearing.

Key term: non-justiciable

Judges do not regard the subject as one on which they can decide.

Lord Diplock also summarised the main bases of judicial review, which can be seen in **Table 4.1**.

Revision tip

This case is often called the GCHQ case and it is worth remembering for its important statements of principle. But later cases have not followed it exactly, so you also need to know about those cases.

Non-justiciable prerogative powers

Despite the judgment in *The Council of Civil Service Unions*, successful judicial reviews of prerogative acts have been rare. The use of many prerogative powers must be left for the government and not the courts to decide. These powers are non-justiciable. There is extensive case law on this area and the courts have refused to consider challenges to government decisions on defence, such as the possession of nuclear weapons or the deployment of troops abroad or foreign policy such as becoming a party to EU treaties.

Prerogative powers subject to judicial review

There have been a few successful challenges to prerogative decisions, where they involved individual rights rather than general government policy. Examples would be the refusal of a passport or a royal pardon. The government may assist UK nationals abroad, but how the government does this is left to its discretion, unless a refusal to help is completely irrational or a severe breach of human rights. The courts have real difficulty if the case is a mixture of individual rights and policies important to the government. For example, the UK government expelled the inhabitants of a British territory, the Chagos Islands, to make way for a US military base. This appears to be a gross breach of human rights, but the UK government argued that their defence and national security interests required it. After a whole series of cases, the Supreme Court finally decided in favour of the government in *R (Bancoult) No 2 v Secretary of State for Foreign Affairs* [2016] UKSC 35. Have a look at **Practice example 4.2** for an illustration of this conflict between policy and individual rights.

Practice example 4.2

Jane is being detained without trial by a foreign government. Her relations want Her Majesty's government to make representations to the foreign government. The government refuses. Can her relatives make the government act?

The court would say that it was irrational for the UK government to do nothing, because it normally would assist UK citizens in this situation. But the court would not specify what the government must do. That would be foreign policy, not individual rights.

We can see the process of judicial review of the prerogative in **Figure 4.1**.

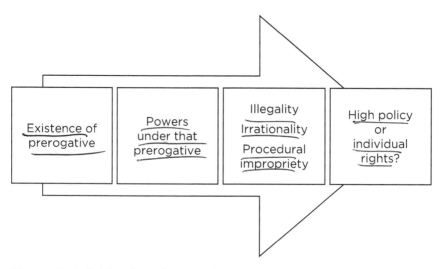

Figure 4.1: Judicial review of the royal prerogative

Summary: judicial review of the royal prerogative	
WHAT is judicial review?	The court will decide whether the government has the power to do what it claims.
WHEN will judicial review be successful?	If the case involves individual rights and not high government policy.

ACCOUNTABILITY TO PARLIAMENT FOR THE PREROGATIVE

This section will help you to revise how Parliament holds the government accountable for prerogative acts. The courts have often explained their refusal to judicially review a prerogative act, by saying that the government must always justify its actions to Parliament and that is a more suitable place to deal with political matters. Unfortunately, there is a long-standing practice of ministers refusing to answer questions on many prerogative powers, which include:

- the prime minister's advice to the King
- the grant of honours
- commercial contracts
- prosecution decisions
- many public appointments (eg judges and bishops)
- confidential discussions with foreign states
- confidential defence and national security issues.

In recent years, the House of Commons has asserted its independence. Since the House of Commons refused to agree to military intervention in Syria in 2013, the government has accepted that the deployment of the armed forces abroad needs to be authorised in advance by a vote of the House. However, the government asserts that there would be exceptions in an emergency or for a humanitarian intervention. Parliament would have the opportunity to consider those deployments afterwards. Look at **Practice example 4.3** for an illustration of Parliament's control over prerogative acts.

Practice example 4.3

A Member of Parliament (MP) strongly disagrees with the sale of armaments to foreign country X. Can the MP do anything to stop this?

The MP can raise the matter in the House of Commons by asking questions or initiating a debate. The government may say that these are confidential issues within the prerogative of defence. The government does not need permission from Parliament to sell arms. Judicial review would not be available for this high policy area of defence.

Exam warning

Questions will normally ask you about the law. But in constitutional law and particularly with questions on the royal prerogative, the question might ask you about convention. Read all questions carefully.

Summary: accountability to Parliament for the prerogative

WHAT is accountability to Parliament?	The government must justify its actions to Parliament.
DOES the government need Parliament's permission?	Usually no.

■ KEY POINT CHECKLIST

This chapter has covered the following key knowledge points. You can use these to structure your revision, making sure to recall the key details for each point, as covered in this chapter.

- The Crown – the legal powers of the King and the government's use of them.
- Crown proceedings.
- Prerogative powers and their identification.
- Acts of Parliament and prerogative powers.
- Highly political prerogative powers may not be judicially reviewed.
- Prerogative powers that affect individual rights may be judicially reviewed.
- The government is accountable to Parliament for its use of prerogative powers.

■ KEY TERMS AND CONCEPTS

- royal prerogative (**page 62**)
- judicial review (**page 68**)
- non-justiciable (**page 69**)

■ SQE1-STYLE QUESTIONS

QUESTION 1

After a general election, no political party has a majority in the House of Commons. The existing prime minister wants to carry on in office.

Which of the following statements best summarises what the monarch should do?

A. The monarch should dismiss the prime minister.

B. The monarch should appoint the leader of the largest political party in the House of Commons as prime minister. ✗

C. The monarch should agree that the prime minister can carry on in office.

D. The monarch should advise the prime minister to form a coalition government of the two largest parties in the House of Commons.

E. The monarch should allow the political parties in the House of Commons to negotiate.

QUESTION 2

A close relative of the monarch is prosecuted for dangerous driving.

Which of the following best summarises the legal position?

A. The relative can be prosecuted, but not sentenced to imprisonment.

B. The relative has immunity from the criminal law.

C. The Crown Proceedings Act 1947 means that the law cannot be enforced against him.

D. By convention, members of the royal family are not prosecuted for minor offences.

E. The relative has no legal immunities or privileges.

QUESTION 3

An overseas possession of the Crown has been invaded by a foreign state. The government decides to send armed forces to recapture the territory. The government requisitions a ship, belonging to a private company, to transport soldiers to the possession and refuses to pay any compensation.

Which of the following best summarises the legal position?

A. The government has no legal power to requisition a ship.

B. The government has the legal power to requisition a ship.

C. The government has the legal power to requisition a ship, but must pay compensation.

D. The government has no legal power to requisition a ship, without the authority of an Act of Parliament.

E. The government has no legal power to requisition a ship, without the permission of Parliament.

QUESTION 4

A man has been refused a passport on the grounds that he is not a UK citizen. He believes that he can prove that he is a UK citizen.

Which of the following best summarises the man's legal position?

A. If the man can prove he is a UK citizen, the government must give him a passport.

B. The man cannot challenge a decision made under the royal prerogative.

C. If the man can prove he is a UK citizen, the government has a discretion to give him a passport.

D. If the man can prove he is a UK citizen, the government must have a valid reason for refusing him a passport.

E. The man cannot challenge the citizenship or the passport decision.

QUESTION 5

A volcanic eruption causes an emergency on a Caribbean island. The prime minister wants to send armed forces to the island to provide humanitarian assistance to the islanders.

Which of the following is the best description of the legal position?

A. The prime minister needs the agreement of the House of Commons.

B. The prime minister needs legislation to authorise this.

C. The prime minister can send the armed forces, but must justify it to the House of Commons.

D. The prime minister needs the agreement of the monarch.

E. The prime minister has the power to do this and does not need any authorisation.

■ ANSWERS TO QUESTIONS

Answers to 'What do you know already?' questions at the start of the chapter

1) The King has kept many legal powers, known as the royal prerogative, which are detailed in the chapter. It is important to remember that the King does not personally use these powers. The government acts in his name.
2) False. It is not possible to sue the King himself, but it is possible to sue the Crown, meaning the government. This is governed by the Crown Proceedings Act 1947.
3) False. The prerogative is a separate source of law to Acts of Parliament. Some prerogative powers have been removed by Acts of Parliament and other prerogatives are duplicated by statutory powers. However, many prerogative powers remain.
4) The correct answer was (a). Prerogative acts that affect individual rights may be reviewable, but prerogatives that involve important political decisions are not.
5) False. The statement is nearly true, because the prerogative allows the government to act and legislate without the authority of Parliament, but the government has conceded that military action normally needs to be authorised by the House of Commons.

Answers to end-of-chapter SQE1-style questions

Question 1:
   The correct answer was E. This is because the convention is that the prime minister should be able to command a majority in the House of Commons. If there is no obvious candidate, the parties in the Commons would be left to negotiate a coalition or minority government. The monarch should not become involved.
Question 2:
   The correct answer was E. This is because only the monarch is above the law. The rest of the royal family have no legal immunities. Be careful. You were asked about the legal position, not about convention.
Question 3:
   The correct answer was C. This because the government has a prerogative power to requisition property for use in military action. Case law states that compensation must be paid.

Question 4:

The correct answer was D. This is because although the granting of a passport is a prerogative power, refusal could be judicially reviewed if there was no legal or rational reason for rejection.

Question 5:

The correct answer was C. This is because a convention has developed in the twenty-first century that the Commons must authorise the deployment of the armed forces abroad for military action. This does not apply to emergencies or humanitarian actions, where the government is merely accountable to Parliament.

■ KEY CASES, RULES, STATUTES AND INSTRUMENTS

The SQE1 Assessment Specification does not require you to remember the *names* of statutes and cases, but you do need to know the principles laid down in the following:

- Crown Proceedings Act 1947 – when the Crown can be sued.
- *M v Home Office* [1994] 1 AC 377 – enforcement of judgments.
- *R (Miller) v The Prime Minister* [2019] UKSC 41 – prorogation of Parliament.
- *Attorney General v De Keyser's Royal Hotel* [1920] AC 508 – statute supersedes prerogative.
- *R (Miller) v Secretary of State for Exiting the European Union* [2017] UKSC 5 – a treaty does not change UK law.
- *R v Secretary of State for the Foreign and Commonwealth Office, ex parte The Council of Civil Service Unions* [1985] AC 374 – judicial review of some prerogatives is possible.

5

Legislation: Primary and secondary

■ MAKE SURE YOU KNOW

This chapter will cover the main aspects of the powers and procedures for the enactment, implementation and repeal of primary and secondary legislation that you will need to know and be able to apply to scenarios, problems and situations for your SQE1 assessment.

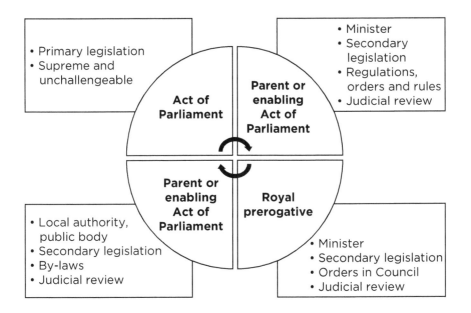

■ SQE ASSESSMENT ADVICE

As you work through this chapter, remember to pay particular attention in your revision to the following:
• the UK Parliament makes primary legislation called Acts of Parliament
• there are two main types of Acts of Parliament: public and private
• parliament lays down its own procedure for passing Acts of Parliament
• parliament can grant law-making powers to others
• this secondary law-making power is limited.

■ WHAT DO YOU KNOW ALREADY?

Have a go at these questions before reading this chapter. If you find some difficult or cannot remember the answers, make a note to look more closely at that subtopic during your revision.

1) In which House of Parliament does a Bill begin its stages?
   a) House of Commons
   b) House of Lords
   c) either House.
   [Acts of Parliament: primary legislation, page 79]

2) What is a private member's Bill?
   a) a Bill introduced by a backbench Member of Parliament (MP)
   b) a Bill introduced by an opposition MP
   c) a Bill introduced by a government minister.
   [The different types of Acts of Parliament, page 79]

3) The King decides when an Act of Parliament comes into force. True or false?
   [The Bill becomes an Act of Parliament, page 83]

4) Which of the following does *not* have the power to make delegated legislation?
   a) government minister
   b) local authority
   c) MP.
   [Types of delegated legislation, page 84]

5) Parliament must vote to approve all delegated legislation. True or false?
   [Parliamentary procedure for delegated legislation, page 85]

6) What is a **Henry VIII clause**?
   a) an Act of Parliament allowing a man to divorce his wife
   b) an Act of Parliament forbidding a Roman Catholic from becoming King or Queen
   c) authority to repeal an Act of Parliament using delegated legislation.
   [Henry VIII clauses, page 87]

ACTS OF PARLIAMENT: PRIMARY LEGISLATION

Parliament is the supreme law-making body for the UK. Parliament can pass an Act of Parliament and make or repeal any law that it wants. This is primary legislation (see **Chapter 2, page 25**).

As part of its sovereignty, Parliament can pass Acts of Parliament granting law-making powers, for specified purposes, to other persons or bodies. This is known as delegated or secondary legislation.

For SQE1 you are required to know about the enactment of primary legislation. This section enables you to revise that topic:
- the different types of Acts of Parliament
- public Bill procedure
- Bills affecting only England or only England and Wales
- Bills in the House of Lords
- private and hybrid Bill procedure
- the Bill becomes an Act of Parliament.

Acts of Parliament start off as Bills. Parliament's own standing orders lay down the procedure for a Bill to become an Act. The Bill must pass through specified stages in both the House of Commons and the House of Lords. Usually, a Bill commences in the House of Commons and, if it is passed by the Commons, proceeds to the House of Lords. Some Bills start in the House of Lords and then go to the House of Commons, particularly if the Bill is uncontroversial or involves law reform. Only Acts of Parliament make law. Other decisions of Parliament, such as a resolution, do not: *Bowles v Bank of England* [1913] 1 Ch 57.

The different types of Acts of Parliament
There are several different types of Acts of Parliament, as can be seen in **Table 5.1**, and they each have a different procedure.

Private member's Bills
Most public Bills are introduced by government ministers. When an ordinary MP introduces a Bill, this is called a private member's Bill. Early in each parliamentary session, MPs may enter a ballot in which 20 MPs are chosen and given the opportunity to introduce a Bill. MPs may also present a Bill under the '10-minute rule' after Prime Minister's Question Time or indeed at any time. The government has a majority of MPs and can therefore control parliamentary business and is unlikely to allow time for a private member's Bill if the government opposes the Bill or if it involves public expenditure. With government support, a few private member's Bills become law.

Table 5.1: Types of parliamentary Bill

Public Bill	Law of general application for all members of society. Generally introduced by a government minister.
Private member's Bill	Also, a public Bill of general application, but introduced by an MP, not the government.
Private Bill	Law for a particular locality, person or persons or body.
Hybrid Bill	Law of general application, but also affects private interests.
Money Bill	The Speaker certifies that the Bill only contains financial measures. The House of Lords does not have to agree to a money Bill.

Exam warning

There are two types of public Bill, those introduced by government ministers and those introduced by ordinary MPs. Remember that a private member's Bill is not the same as a private Bill.

Public Bill procedure

Before the government introduces a Bill, it is likely to have consulted widely. It might issue a Green Paper, setting out possible policies and inviting comment and then a White Paper, which contains more definite proposals. Parliamentary draftsmen (parliamentary counsel) put the policies into legal language and then the Bill is approved by the Cabinet Home Affairs Committee. A government minister will be chosen to pilot the Bill through its various parliamentary stages, which are shown in **Table 5.2**.

Under the UK system, the government has a majority of MPs, so a Bill is usually approved with few amendments. The important, controversial Bills take up most of parliamentary time with the other Bills being passed quickly. The majority controls the time spent discussing each Bill and a programme motion is usually passed, allocating the time to be spent on each stage. If there is an emergency, Bills can go through all their stages very quickly, if the House votes for the 'fast-track procedure'. For example, the European Union (Future Relationship) Act 2020 became law in one day.

Table 5.2: Parliamentary stages in the House of Commons

Pre-legislative scrutiny	A select committee may undertake further consultations on the Bill. The Joint Committee on Human Rights checks for compatibility with human rights.
First reading	The name of the Bill is announced.
Second reading	Debate and vote upon whether the Bill should go forward.
Committee stage	A Public Bill Committee of 18–25 MPs, in proportion to party strength, considers the Bill in detail. Amendments may be made. The whole House might form the Committee for important Bills.
Report stage	The Bill comes back to the full House, which decides whether to accept any amendments made in committee.
Third reading	Minor mistakes are corrected, and the Bill is approved.

Bills affecting only England or only England and Wales

Scotland, Wales and Northern Ireland have their own legislatures, so when a Bill only affects the law in England or England and Wales there is an extra stage, after the report stage. The Speaker of the House of Commons certifies that the Bill only affects English law or English and Welsh law. Then a Grand Committee consisting only of MPs representing English constituencies, or English and Welsh constituencies, considers the Bill and may reject it.

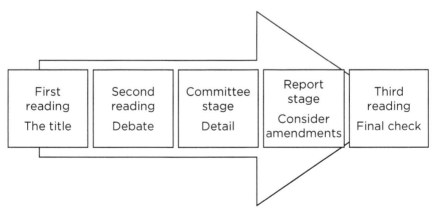

Figure 5.1: The stages of a parliamentary Bill

Bills in the House of Lords

Once a Bill has been approved by the House of Commons, it must go through the same stages in the House of Lords, or in the Commons, if the Bill started in the Lords. In the Lords, the committee stage is taken by the whole House rather than a small committee of members. Because no political party has a majority in the House of Lords, there will be a more detailed discussion of the Bill. The House of Commons may accept amendments made by the Lords, but as the Commons could use the Parliament Acts 1911 and 1949 to bypass the need for the Lords to agree, the Lords would usually back down if the Commons did not accept their amendments. Under the Parliament Acts the Commons may wait a year and pass the Bill for a second time and then it goes for royal assent.

Private and hybrid Bill procedure

The procedure for private Bills is a little different. Organisations such as local authorities or companies, who want more legal powers, will appoint a parliamentary agent (specialist firms of lawyers) to pilot the Bill through Parliament. Notice must be served on those affected, such as landowners, and local meetings may be called. There are further opportunities for those affected to object and argue against the Bill at the Committee stage. Hybrid Bills have a similar procedure where objections can be made. Whether the correct procedure has been followed is decided by Parliament. The courts will not intervene, as shown in *R (HS2 Action Alliance Ltd) v Secretary of State for Transport* [2014] UKSC 3. Two hybrid Bills were required to build the high-speed railway, because, although it was a national project, it also took land from private owners. The Supreme Court would not accept any claim that Parliament had not followed the correct procedure. Look at **Practice example 5.1** for an illustration of this.

Practice example 5.1

A Public Act of Parliament has gone through all its stages in the House of Commons and the House of Lords, except that it did not have a third reading in the Lords. The Act received the royal assent. Would it still be law?

Yes. The court would not investigate any claims that there were defects in parliamentary procedure. As a sovereign body it would be solely up to Parliament what, if anything, to do about the procedural defect.

The Bill becomes an Act of Parliament

Usually, all the stages of a Bill must be completed within a parliamentary session or the process must start again in the next session of Parliament. However, government Bills may be carried over once from one session to another.

Once a Bill has passed all its stages in Parliament, it is given the royal assent. The King plays no personal role in this procedure, the names of the new Bills are just read out in Parliament. The new Act will contain a section that states the date when it comes **into force** or more commonly it will delegate power to a government minister to issue an order or regulation stating when the Act comes into force. It is common for different parts of an Act to come into force at different times. It is possible for parts of an Act or the whole Act to never be brought into force (eg the Easter Act 1928).

Key term: into force

Just because an Act has been passed by Parliament does not mean that it is the law. It must also be brought into force.

Revision tip

Remember that all parliamentary Bills, of whatever kind, must pass through the same stages in Parliament. The royal assent is a formality, but most Acts of Parliament do not come into force immediately; they are brought into force in stages by order of government ministers.

Summary: Acts of Parliament

WHAT is an Act of Parliament?	The only form of primary legislation.
HOW is it made?	It must pass through the procedures laid down by Parliament.

Acts of Senedd Cymru

As discussed in Chapter 3, the UK Parliament has devolved its law-making powers in a number of subject areas to the Senedd. It is important to note that legislation which is passed by the Senedd can only apply to Wales, whereas Acts of Parliament which extend to England and Wales may apply in relation to both England and Wales, only in relation to England, or only in relation to Wales.

All Acts of Senedd Cymru begin life as Bills. Once a Bill has been considered and passed by the Senedd, and given Royal Assent by the monarch, it becomes an Act of Senedd Cymru. Bills may be introduced by the Welsh Government, a Senedd Committee, an individual Member or the Senedd Commission. Generally speaking, a Bill passes through four stages before it becomes an Act of Senedd Cymru. The process is summarised below:

- Stage 1: The Senedd considers and agrees the general principles of the Bill.
- Stage 2: A committee scrutinises the Bill and proposes any amendments to it.
- Stage 3: The Senedd scrutinises the Bill and proposes any amendments to it.
- Stage 4: The Senedd votes to pass the final text of the Bill.

DELEGATED LEGISLATION (SECONDARY LEGISLATION)

An enabling or parent Act of Parliament grants to a person or body the power to make law. Many modern Acts of Parliament only give an outline or framework, with the detail to be filled in later by delegated legislation. This is done because Parliament lacks the time or detailed knowledge or wants the ability to change the law rapidly, for example the Coronavirus Act 2020. Parliament passes fewer than 100 new Acts of Parliament a year, but around 3,500 pieces of delegated legislation. SQE1 requires you to know about secondary legislation, so in this section you will be able to revise:

- types of delegated legislation
- parliamentary procedure for delegated legislation
- delegated legislation affecting only England or only England and Wales
- Henry VIII clauses (see later in chapter)
- judicial review of delegated legislation.

Types of delegated legislation

There are several types of delegated legislation. The enabling Act specifies which sort of secondary legislation may be made:

- Many Acts of Parliament give government ministers, usually the secretary of state, the power to make rules, regulations and orders.
- Some Acts give government ministers, usually the secretary of state, the power to make Orders in Council. These are used for important matters, such as constitutional changes. The Council is the Privy Council, which is merely a ceremonial body nowadays.
- The King retains a power to make Orders in Council using his prerogative powers. Government ministers act in his name (see **Chapter 4, page 65**).
- The Supreme Court has the power to make its own rules of procedure.

These first four categories are statutory instruments, governed by the Statutory Instruments Act 1946. They are referenced by year and number (eg SI 1977/352). There are other types of delegated legislation that are not statutory instruments. These are:

- The Provisional Collection of Taxes Act 1968 allows a resolution of the House of Commons, changing taxes in the budget, to have statutory effect until the annual Finance Act can be passed.
- Many public bodies have been given the power to make their own rules and regulations. Many professional bodies have the power to make Orders of Council.
- Local authorities (councils) have been granted the power to make by-laws for their area. Section 235 of the Local Government Act 1972 allows councils to make by-laws 'for good rule and government and the suppression of nuisances'. These must be approved by the secretary of state for housing, communities and local government.

Delegated legislation is made by the executive not the legislature. Look at **Practice example 5.2**, which illustrates this.

Practice example 5.2

A client is very concerned about a planned Order in Council, which she considers will affect her business. She wants to petition the King to make her objections.

This would be pointless. The King and his Privy Council only play a ceremonial role in approving this secondary legislation. Your client needs to make her objections to the government department and minister who will actually decide.

Parliamentary procedure for delegated legislation

There are several different procedures to make delegated legislation law and the parent Act specifies which one must be followed. SQE1 requires that you know the procedures for laying before Parliament, negative resolution and affirmative resolution (**Figure 5.2**).

Laying before Parliament

The legislation is **laid** before Parliament. This means that it is brought to the attention of MPs in their daily list of votes and proceedings. It becomes law unless MPs object. This procedure is used for Commencement Regulations and Orders in Council.

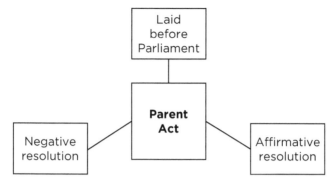

Figure 5.2: Approval of delegated legislation

Key term: laid

The proposed delegated legislation is brought to the attention of MPs. This is an essential procedural requirement.

Negative resolution procedure

The delegated legislation becomes law unless Parliament votes against it. There are two versions of this procedure:

- The legislation is law when made but a resolution of either House, within 40 days, may annul it.
- The legislation is laid in draft, but a resolution of either House, within 40 days, prevents it becoming made (law).

Affirmative resolution procedure

The Houses of Parliament must approve the legislation. There are three versions of this procedure:

- The legislation is laid in draft and the draft must be approved by a resolution of both Houses (only the Commons for financial matters) before it is made (becomes law).
- The legislation is made (is law) but cannot come into force until it is approved by a resolution of both Houses.
- The legislation is made (is law) and comes into force immediately but lapses unless it is approved by a resolution of both Houses within a specified period. Typically, this is 28 or 40 days.

Exam warning

Acts of Parliament all have the same parliamentary procedure, but there are different procedures for delegated legislation, depending upon what the parent Act requires.

Delegated legislation affecting only England or only England and Wales

As with parliamentary Bills, if the delegated legislation only affects English law or English and Welsh law, MPs representing English constituencies, or English and Welsh constituencies, consider the legislation and may reject it.

Although Parliament spends more time debating delegated legislation nowadays, it is very unusual for it to reject the legislation, whichever procedure is used. If the parent Act is later repealed, the secondary legislation made under it ceases to have effect.

Henry VIII clauses

Some Acts of Parliament contain sections that allow ministers to amend or repeal provisions in an Act of Parliament using delegated legislation. These are known as **Henry VIII clauses** and are controversial because they allow the executive to make law rather than the legislature.

> **Key term: Henry VIII clause**
>
> Gives a minister the power to change an Act of Parliament using delegated legislation. King Henry VIII preferred to legislate by royal proclamation, rather than Act of Parliament.

Acts of Parliament that contain such clauses may provide greater powers for Parliament to approve delegated legislation made under them. This is the super-affirmative procedure, where Parliament has 60 days to consider the measure. The Human Rights Act 1998 is an example of this. It allows the making of Remedial Orders, when a court has made a declaration of incompatibility and part of an Act of Parliament must be changed to comply (see **Chapter 8, page 138** for s 10 Human Rights Act 1998).

> **Revision tip**
>
> Henry VIII clauses are worth remembering. They are not just used under the Human Rights Act, but also the European Communities Act 1972 and European Union (Withdrawal) Act 2018. You can read more about those two Acts in **Chapter 9**.

Judicial review of delegated legislation

The sovereignty of Parliament means that the courts will not accept any challenge to the validity of an Act of Parliament (see **Chapter 2,**

page 25 for this principle). However, the validity of all types of delegated legislation may be questioned using the process of judicial review and the legislation may be declared invalid. The court will closely inspect the wording of the parent Act and decide whether the delegated legislation goes beyond what is permitted under the Act (ultra vires). Judicial review would be under the three main grounds of illegality, irrationality and procedural impropriety laid out in *Council of Civil Service Unions v Minister for the Civil Service* [1985] AC 374. The Human Rights Act 1998 added breach of human rights (see **Chapter 8** for more information). **Table 5.3** gives you an overview of when a judicial review would be successful. You do not need to remember the case names, but the principles are important.

Table 5.3: Successful judicial review of delegated legislation

R (Public Law Project) v Lord Chancellor [2016] UKSC 34	Illegality	The Lord Chancellor did not have the power to add a residence requirement for legal aid when the parent Act did not require it.
R (Javed) v Secretary of State for the Home Department [2001] EWCA Civ 789	Irrationality	The home secretary designated Pakistan as a safe country to which to deport asylum seekers, despite the evidence to the contrary.
Agricultural, Horticultural and Forestry Training Board v Aylesbury Mushrooms [1972] 1 WLR 190	Procedural impropriety	Many Acts have consultation requirements before the delegated legislation is made. The consultation must be genuine.
R (Alvi) v Secretary of State for the Home Department [2012] 1 WLR 2208	Procedural impropriety	The parliamentary procedure for approval in the parent Act had not been followed.
Ahmed v HM Treasury [2010] UKSC 2	Breach of human rights	Ahmed was not given a hearing before an Order in Council froze his assets.

Judicial review is possible even if the legislation has been agreed by Parliament under the affirmative resolution procedure, as seen in *Javed* and *Public Law Project*. See **Practice example 5.3** for how a court might interpret the powers granted in an Act of Parliament to make delegated legislation.

Practice example 5.3

Section 96 of the Terrorism Act 2000 states that 'the secretary of state may by regulations make provision for promoting the preservation of the peace and the maintenance of order'. Would this give the secretary of state the power to make regulations for imprisoning suspected terrorists without trial?

No, it would be illegal. The wording of s 96 would need to specifically allow this, because it would also be a breach of human rights.

Summary: delegated legislation

WHAT is delegated legislation?	Secondary legislation made under the authority of Act of Parliament.
WHO is it used by?	Government ministers, local authorities and public bodies.
WHAT power do they have to legislate?	Only the power granted by the Act of Parliament.

■ KEY POINT CHECKLIST

This chapter has covered the following key knowledge points. You can use these to structure your revision, making sure to recall the key details for each point, as covered in this chapter.

- Parliament makes primary legislation known as Acts of Parliament.
- Parliament decides its own procedure for parliamentary Bills.
- The Parliament Acts limit the powers of the House of Lords.
- Acts of Parliament grant secondary law-making powers (delegated legislation).
- Parliament may approve delegated legislation.
- Acts of Parliament cannot be judicially reviewed, but delegated legislation can.

Can be judicially review delegated legislation BUT NOT primary Acts of Parliament.

■ KEY TERMS AND CONCEPTS

- into force (**page 83**)
- laid (**page 86**)
- Henry VIII clause (**page 87**)

■ SQE1-STYLE QUESTIONS

QUESTION 1

A client is being tried for an offence under an Act of Parliament that was not in force on the date when the offence was committed.

Which of the following decisions would the court make?

A. The court would declare the Act of Parliament void.

B. The court would order Parliament to either bring the Act into force or repeal it.

C. The court would acquit the client.

D. The court would make a declaration of incompatibility under the Human Rights Act 1998.

E. The court would convict the client.

QUESTION 2

The largest political party in the House of Lords is opposed to a Bill that has passed all its stages in the House of Commons and wants to prevent this Bill from becoming law.

Which of the following statements best summarises the legal position?

A. The House of Lords can vote against the Bill and prevent it becoming law.

B. The House of Lords can only amend the Bill, but not prevent it from becoming law.

C. The House of Lords may refer the Bill to a Joint Committee of the Commons and Lords.

D. The House of Lords may delay the Bill, but not prevent it from becoming law.

E. The House of Lords can vote against the Bill and then royal assent will be refused.

QUESTION 3

A haulage firm objects to some new regulations made by the secretary of state for transport. They have been approved by both Houses of Parliament, but the haulage firm can prove that the enabling Act does not give the secretary of state the power to make these regulations. The firm seeks a judicial review.

Which of the following best summarises the legal position?

A. The secretary of state has an inherent power to make regulations.

B. The secretary of state may use the royal prerogative to make regulations.

C. The secretary of state's regulations have been approved by Parliament and are legal.

D. The secretary of state's regulations are illegal and void.

E. The secretary of state's regulations cannot be judicially reviewed.

QUESTION 4

In a court case, the Supreme Court has declared that a particular section of an Act of Parliament is incompatible with the human rights protected under the Human Rights Act 1998. The secretary of state for home affairs wishes to remove the incompatibility as soon as possible.

Which of the following courses of action would take the least time?

A. The secretary of state could ask Parliament to repeal the offending Act of Parliament.

B. The secretary of state could ask Parliament to amend the offending Act of Parliament.

C. The secretary of state could ask the Supreme Court to reconsider the case.

D. The secretary of state could ask Parliament to repeal the Human Rights Act 1998.

E. The secretary of state could ask Parliament to make a Remedial Order.

QUESTION 5

A new set of regulations has been made by the secretary of state using a statutory power that requires the affirmative resolution procedure. The House of Commons and the House of Lords have not voted to approve these regulations. A client wishes to judicially review these regulations.

Which of the following best summarises the legal position?

A. The court would declare the regulations void for procedural impropriety.

B. The court would declare the regulations valid, as minor defects in procedure are immaterial.

C. The court would refer the regulations back to Parliament for approval.

D. The court would refuse to judicially review legislation.

E. The court would ask the secretary of state to confirm that he approves the regulations.

■ ANSWERS TO QUESTIONS

Answers to 'What do you know already?' questions at the start of the chapter

1) The correct answer was (c). Most Bills start in the Commons, but they can also start in the Lords.

2) The correct answer was (a). Any MP may introduce a Bill, but there is little chance of it becoming law without government support.

3) False. Either the Act itself states when it becomes law, or the Act will give a minister the power to bring it into force.

4) The correct answer was (c). Delegated legislation is made by the government, not ordinary MPs.

5) False. Only the Affirmative Resolution requires this.

6) The correct answer (c). An Act of Parliament can give a minister the power to repeal or amend an Act, using delegated legislation.

Answers to end-of-chapter SQE1-style questions

Question 1:
The correct answer was C. This is because if an Act of Parliament is not in force it is not the law. It is a basic principle of statutory interpretation that an Act of Parliament is not retrospective unless it explicitly says so.

Question 2:
The correct answer was D. This is because the House of Lords cannot prevent the House of Commons passing an Act, but only delay the

Commons for a year. Usually, the two Houses compromise and agree amendments, because the government does not want to wait a year for its legislation.

Question 3:

The correct answer was D. This is because there must be a power under an enabling or parent Act, which allows the secretary of state to make the regulations. Without such a power, Parliament's approval is irrelevant.

Question 4:

The correct answer was E. This is because there is a 'fast-track' procedure under s 10 of the Human Rights Act 1998, where a Remedial Order may be made that can repeal or amend an Act of Parliament. As it is delegated legislation, it does not have to go through the numerous stages required for a parliamentary Bill.

Question 5:

The correct answer was A. This is because procedural impropriety is one of the bases of judicial review. Failure to comply with the laying requirements laid down in the parent Act might lead to the court declaring the regulations void.

■ KEY CASES, RULES, STATUTES AND INSTRUMENTS

The SQE1 Assessment Specification does not require you to remember the names of statutes and cases, but you do need to know the principles laid down in the following:

• *R (HS2 Action Alliance Ltd) v Secretary of State for Transport* [2014] UKSC 3 – the courts cannot question the procedure used to pass an Act of Parliament.

• *R (Public Law Project) v Lord Chancellor* [2016] UKSC 34 – the courts can judicially review delegated legislation for defective procedure.

6

Public order law

■ MAKE SURE YOU KNOW

This chapter will cover the main aspects of public order law – processions, assemblies and **breach of the peace** – that you will need to know and be able to apply to scenarios, problems and situations for your SQE1 assessment.

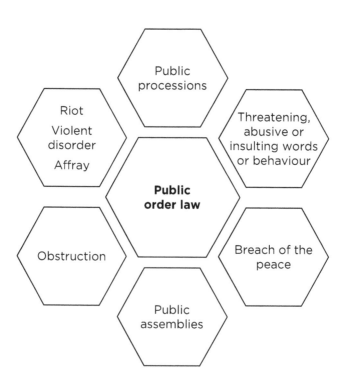

■ SQE ASSESSMENT ADVICE

As you work through this chapter, remember to pay particular attention in your revision to:
• the definition of a public procession and police powers
• the definition of a public assembly and police powers
• the definition of breach of the peace and police powers
• the criminal offences used to keep public order.

■ WHAT DO YOU KNOW ALREADY?

Have a go at these questions before reading this chapter. If you find some difficult or cannot remember the answers, make a note to look more closely at that subtopic during your revision

1) Who has the power to ban a public procession?
   a) the chief officer of police
   b) the council of the district
   c) the secretary of state.
   [Public processions, page 96]

2) How many persons are required for a public assembly?
   a) 2
   b) 12
   c) 20.
   [Public assemblies, page 97]

3) A breach of the peace is
   a) excessive noise
   b) violence
   c) anti-social behaviour.
   [Definition of breach of the peace, page 100]

4) Using their breach of the peace power, the police may detain a person without arresting them or charging them with any offence. True or false.
   [Breach of the peace: enforcement, page 102]

5) Which is the most serious public order offence?
   [Public order offences, page 103]

6) The Criminal Justice and Public Order Act 1994 criminalised certain forms of trespass, such as trespassory assembly, raves and aggravated trespass. What do these offences have in common?
   a) they might cause violence
   b) they disrupt the lives of others
   c) they involve large numbers of people.
   [Processions and assemblies, page 96; aggravated trespass, page 106]

INTRODUCTION TO PUBLIC ORDER LAW

Public order law is found in several sources. There is the old common law of **breach of the peace**, added to by legislation such as the Public Order Act (POA) 1986 and the Criminal Justice and Public Order Act (CJPOA) 1994. There is some duplication, with the police often having different powers to deal with the same situation. The Human Rights Act (HRA) 1998 must also be considered. Article 10 of the European Convention on Human Rights (ECHR) guarantees that 'everyone has the right to freedom of expression', but that right may be restricted 'for the prevention of disorder or crime'. Article 11 provides that 'everyone has the right to freedom of peaceful assembly' but is also restricted 'for the prevention of disorder and crime'.

PROCESSIONS AND ASSEMBLIES

SQE1 requires a knowledge of the law relating to assemblies and processions, so you need to know how to distinguish between them. Processions or marches are thought to be a more serious threat to public order than a public assembly or static demonstration and so are more strictly regulated. In this section you will be able to revise:
- public processions
- public assemblies
- trespassory assemblies
- raves.

Public processions

There is no statutory definition of 'public procession', but, logically, it must involve more than one person moving along a route. It must be in a place to which the public has access or any highway. Sections 11–13 of the POA 1986 provide that:
- The organisers must give written notice of a public procession demonstrating support or opposition, publicising a cause or commemorating an event to a police station at least six days in advance, giving the date, time, route and the names of the organisers.
  - This is not required if it is not reasonably practicable or it is a common or customary event or a funeral.
- If the senior officer of police reasonably believes that the procession may result in serious public disorder, serious damage to property or serious disruption to the life of the community or that the purpose

of the organisers is to intimidate others, then the officer may give directions to the organisers or those taking part, including conditions on the route or restrictions on entering any public place.

- If the chief officer of police reasonably believes that these powers will not be sufficient to prevent serious public disorder, he/she shall apply to the local council for an order prohibiting the holding of all public processions in the district or part of a district for a maximum of three months. The consent of the secretary of state for home affairs is required for the order. In London, the commissioner of police of the metropolis applies directly to the secretary of state.

It is an offence to fail to notify or to disobey police conditions.

Exam warning

When an event is held regularly and it is considered common or customary, the organisers do not need to give written notice to the police. For example, in *R (Kay) v Commissioner of Police of the Metropolis* [2008] UKHL 69, a mass protest cycle ride in London was held to be a public procession, but as it was held monthly, it had become customary and did not have to be notified to the police.

Public assemblies

Assemblies or demonstrations are regulated by s 14 of the POA 1986 and defined as 'an assembly of two or more persons in a public place which is wholly or partly open to the air'.

If the senior officer of police reasonably believes that the assembly may result in serious public disorder, serious damage to property or serious disruption to the life of the community or that the purpose of the organisers is to intimidate others, then the officer may give directions to the organisers or those taking part, including conditions such as the place the assembly is held, its maximum duration or the maximum numbers of persons. It is an offence to disobey police conditions.

Although the police have power to control individual assemblies, unlike with processions, there is no power to ban *all* assemblies in the district: *R (Jones) v Commissioner of Police of the Metropolis (Extinction Rebellion)* [2019] EWHC 2957 (Admin). Have a look at **Table 6.1** to help you distinguish between processions and assemblies.

Table 6.1: Processions compared to assemblies

Public procession	Public assembly
Highway or where the public have access	Where the public have access in the open air
No statutory minimum	Minimum of two people
Organisers must notify police	No statutory duty to notify police
Serious public disorder, serious damage to property, serious disruption to the life of the community, intimidation	Serious public disorder, serious damage to property, serious disruption to the life of the community, intimidation
Conditions on the route or restrictions on entering any public place	Conditions on place, duration and number
Three-month ban on all processions in the district	No statutory power to ban

Exam warning

In a real-life situation it might be difficult to distinguish between a procession and an assembly, but legally they are regarded as quite different. Read the facts given in a question and apply the criteria laid out in **Table 6.1** to decide which you are being asked about.

Trespassory assemblies

The CJPOA 1994 added powers to control trespassory assemblies to the POA 1986. A trespassory assembly:

• is an assembly of 20 or more persons on land in the open air
• is held on land to which the public has no or only limited right of access for a particular purpose, such as a highway or road, and it is likely that the occupier will not have given permission
• may result in serious disruption to the life of the community or
• significant damage to the land, buildings or monument of historical, architectural, archaeological or scientific importance.

If the chief officer of police reasonably believes that a trespassory assembly is intended, he may apply to the council of the district for an order prohibiting all trespassory assemblies in the district. The secretary of state for home affairs must consent. In London, the commissioner of police of the metropolis applies directly to the secretary of state.

• The order may not exceed four days or a five-mile radius from a specified centre.

• The organisers and those taking part commit an offence and the police may stop people proceeding to a trespassory assembly.

It is essential to prove that there is a trespass. In *DPP v Jones (Margaret) and Another* [1999] 2 AC 240, 21 people were standing on the roadside verge adjacent to the perimeter fence of Stonehenge protesting about a banned festival. They were acquitted because they were not trespassing. Their use of the highway was reasonable. They were causing no obstruction and there was a right of peaceful assembly on the highway. Look at **Practice example 6.1** for another illustration of police powers over assemblies and processions.

Practice example 6.1

A protest group plans to hold meetings at 20 underground stations in London. The police fear that commuters will object to having their journeys home interrupted. Can the police stop these meetings?

No. These are public assemblies and not public processions. There is no power to ban all the meetings: *R (Jones) v Commissioner of Police of the Metropolis (Extinction Rebellion)* [2019] EWHC 2957 (Admin). Police could attend each meeting and use their powers to control public assemblies there.

Raves

The CJ and POA 1994 also gives a police superintendent the power to disperse a rave and stop persons travelling to a rave within five miles of the boundary of a rave site. The police also have the power to seize vehicles and sound equipment. A rave is defined as follows:

• A gathering of 20 or more persons on land in the open air without an entertainment licence. If it is in a building, they must be trespassers.

• Amplified music is played during the night.

• The loudness and duration of the music is likely to cause serious distress to the inhabitants of the locality.

Summary: processions and assemblies

WHAT is the difference between a procession and an assembly?	A procession is a moving demonstration and an assembly is stationary.
WHAT difference does this make?	The police have greater powers to control a procession than an assembly.
WHAT is the problem?	To allow protest but prevent violence and disorder.

BREACH OF THE PEACE

SQE1 requires you to know about the ancient common-law concept of **breach of the peace**. All citizens and particularly police officers have a duty to maintain the peace of the realm. In this section you will be able to revise:

• the definition of breach of the peace
• controlling a breach of the peace
• human rights and breach of the peace
• enforcement of breach of the peace.

Key term: breach of the peace

Breach of the peace involves violence or a threat of violence and includes provoking others to violence.

Definition of breach of the peace

There are two aspects to the modern definition of breach of the peace:
• 'An act done or threatened to be done which actually harms a person, or in his presence his property, or is likely to cause such harm or which puts someone in fear of such harm being done' (taken from *R v Howell (Erroll)* [1982] 2 QB 416).
• Conduct that has the natural consequence of provoking others to violence.

The police may need to act before the violence occurs as explained in *Moss v McLachlan* [1985] IRLR 76: 'Provided the police honestly and reasonably formed the opinion that there was a real risk of a breach of the peace in the sense that it was in close proximity both in place and time, then the conditions existed for reasonable preventative action.'

Controlling a breach of the peace

The police may do anything that is reasonable to prevent a breach of the peace, and this gives them several legal powers, for example:

• power to ban a procession
• power to disperse an assembly
• power to enter private premises
• power to detain people
• power to prevent people travelling
• power to remove provocative signs or emblems.

Revision tip

Breach of the peace gives police powers that they also possess under public order legislation. Consider scenarios carefully to distinguish whether they are about the statutory or common-law position.

Human rights and breach of the peace

The Human Rights Act 1998 has affected the interpretation of police powers. Protest should be permitted, if it does not cause violence. In *Redmond-Bate v Director of Public Prosecutions* [2000] HRLR 249, the public preaching of three Christian fundamentalists attracted a hostile crowd. A police officer asked the speakers to stop and when they refused, he arrested them. The arrest was unlawful because the defendants had a right to free expression under Article 10 ECHR. Their speech might be offensive to others, but was lawful, if it did not tend to provoke violence. The police officer should have dealt with members of the crowd threatening or causing violence. Similarly, in *R (Laporte) v Chief Constable of Gloucestershire* [2007] 2 AC 105, it was unlawful to stop people travelling from London to Gloucestershire to protest, because there was not enough evidence that violence was imminent.

Yet the police retain the power to detain, if there is evidence that there could be violence, as shown in *Austin v Commissioner of Police for the Metropolis* [2009] UKHL 5, where 3,000 people, many of whom were not protesters, were detained for seven hours. The police action was reasonable and proportionate, justifying the restriction of the Article 5 ECHR right to liberty and security of the person. These mass detentions are known as 'kettling'.

Look at **Practice example 6.2** for how breach of the peace works.

Practice example 6.2

A large anti-war protest meeting has been organised in City Hall. The police fear that opponents will try to disrupt the meeting. What powers do the police have?

This is not a public assembly under the POA 1986 as it is indoors, but the police could use their breach of the peace powers to enter the hall. They should not stop the meeting, but should attempt to control the potentially violent opponents.

Breach of the peace: enforcement

Breach of the peace is not a crime, although it carries a power of arrest. Sometimes the arrested are freed without charge, although they can be bound over to keep the peace or prosecuted for obstruction of a police officer or, if the breach of the peace was on the highway, obstruction of the highway.

Binding over

Binding over to keep the peace is a civil remedy, but with a criminal standard of proof. The court must be satisfied that a breach of the peace has occurred and that there is a real risk of violence in the future. The court must identify the specific conduct or activity from which the individual must refrain. Usually the order would not exceed 12 months and the defendant can be asked to pay a specified sum if they break the order (a recognisance). If they refuse to be bound over, they can be imprisoned for up to six months.

Key term: binding over

A magistrate or judge may order a defendant to refrain from certain specified conduct for a particular period of time.

To bind someone over, the court must be satisfied that the defendant is likely to repeat their violent conduct, as illustrated in *Percy v DPP* [1995] 1 WLR 1382. The defendant had protested by repeatedly climbing the fence into a military air base. She was not violent and there was no evidence that her actions were likely to provoke trained military personnel to a violent response. There were no grounds to bind her over.

Obstruction of a police officer (s 89 Police Act 1996)

If a person refuses the reasonable direction of a police officer, legitimately trying to prevent a breach of the peace, they commit the offence of obstructing a constable in the execution of their duty. In *Duncan v Jones* [1936] 1 KB 218, the defendants were convicted for refusing to disperse a public meeting when a police officer asked.

Obstruction of the highway (s 137 Highways Act 1980)

Many meetings and marches take place on the public highway, which includes the pavement. The normal use of the highway is for passage and repassage. Wilful obstruction of the highway without lawful excuse is an offence. Protests involving small numbers of people on the highway are lawful, as the highway is not actually blocked and there is a right to protest: *DPP v Jones (Margaret) and Another* [1999] 2 AC 240.

Summary: breach of the peace	
WHAT is breach of the peace?	A common-law power to control violence or threats of violence.
WHAT does it allow the police to do?	To take any reasonable step to prevent imminent threats of violence.

PUBLIC ORDER OFFENCES

Some criminal offences are specifically designed to control public order. Sections 1–5 of the POA 1986 have five criminal offences directed at public order, from the most serious, riot, with 10 years imprisonment, to the non-imprisonable offence of causing harassment, alarm or distress. All the offences may be committed in a public or private place and intent (mens rea) must be proved for each one. The offences you will be able to revise in this section are:

- riot
- violent disorder
- affray
- fear or provocation of violence
- harassment, alarm or distress
- aggravated trespass.

Riot

Riot is a multi-part offence and all the elements listed in **Table 6.2** must be proved.

Table 6.2: Elements of a riot

12 or more persons present together	The group must be using or threatening unlawful violence.
Use or threaten unlawful violence	This is violence to persons or property and includes throwing missiles.
For a common purpose	This does not have to be pre-planned, but requires the 12 people to support each other in the violence or threats of violence.
Cause a person of reasonable firmness present at the scene to fear for their safety	This is a standard of reasonableness. There is no need to prove that someone present was actually scared.
Using unlawful violence for a common purpose	The defendants must use violence, not just threaten it, to be guilty of riot.

Violent disorder

Violent disorder has similar elements to riot, but only requires three people and does not require a common purpose. The offence is committed not just by those who use violence, but also those who threaten violence. It must also cause a person of reasonable firmness present at the scene to fear for their safety. In *R v Fleming* [1989] Crim LR 658, two defendants could not be convicted of violent disorder, because there must be at least three persons using or threatening violence. But they could be convicted of affray.

Affray

Affray also has several elements:
• one or two persons acting together
• use or threaten unlawful violence – this cannot be words alone
• cause a person of reasonable firmness present at the scene to fear for their safety.

According to *R v Sanchez* [1996] Crim LR 572, this offence envisages at least three people – the person committing the violence, their victim and a bystander. The court would look at all the circumstances to determine whether it was reasonable for a bystander to be fearful.

Exam warning

Note that there are subtle differences between the different offences in the POA 1986. Which offence are you being asked about?

Look at **Practice example 6.3** for an illustration of the differences between these first three offences.

Practice example 6.3

A football match has just ended. United have beaten City and disgruntled City supporters leave the ground, smashing shop windows and looting the contents. Which public order offences have been committed?

Riot would be difficult to prove with separate groups of supporters. That offence requires at least 12 people and they might not be acting for a common purpose. Affray does not include violence against property, but violent disorder does. Violent disorder also only requires three people and does not require a common purpose.

Revision tip

Public order law involves minimum numbers for offences and to trigger police powers. **Figure 6.1** might help you remember.

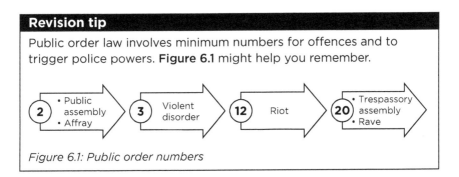

Figure 6.1: Public order numbers

Fear or provocation of violence (s 4)

Fear or provocation of violence has two main elements. First, a person must be subjected to:

- threatening, abusive or insulting words or behaviour or
- threatening, abusive or insulting writing, sign or other visible representation.

Revision tip

The words 'threatening, abusive or insulting' have no technical legal meaning, but are what the ordinary person would understand by them.

But there must also be an intent:

- to cause that person to believe that unlawful violence will be used against them or
- to provoke the immediate use of unlawful violence.

The provocation of violence need not be instantaneous but there must be proximity in time and causation: *R v Horseferry Road Justices* [1991] 1 All ER 324.

Harassment, alarm or distress (s 5)

Harassment, alarm or distress also has two main elements. First a person uses:

- threatening, abusive or insulting words or behaviour or
- threatening, abusive or insulting writing, sign or other visible representation or
- disorderly behaviour.

But the words or behaviour must be within the hearing or sight of a person likely to be caused harassment, alarm or distress. Whether someone is likely to be harassed, alarmed or distressed is a question of fact. Swearing at police officers is unlikely to be an offence, as they are used to it: *DPP v Orum* [1988] 3 All ER 449. Defacing the flag of the USA, might be insulting to US service personnel, but the right of free expression (Article 10 ECHR) outweighs this: *Percy v DPP* [2002] Crim LR 835. Look at **Practice example 6.4** for how this offence could be applied.

Practice example 6.4

A woman is walking home, alone, at night. A man follows her, shouting and making indecent suggestions. The woman asks him to stop but he persists, so the woman complains to a police officer. Is there any offence for which the police officer may arrest the man?

Yes, causing harassment, alarm or distress is an offence under s 5 POA 1986. The man's words could be considered threatening, abusive or insulting or his behaviour disorderly, and it would be reasonable for the woman to consider herself to be harassed, alarmed or distressed in these circumstances.

Aggravated trespass

Section 68 of the CJPOA 1994 makes it an offence to trespass on land with intent to disrupt, obstruct or intimidate those engaged in a lawful activity. A senior officer of police may direct those committing or about to commit this offence to leave the land. The prosecution must prove that the defendants are not just trespassing, but are engaged in acts to disrupt the lawful activity. *R v Jones* [2006] UKHL 16 is a good example of the type of conduct covered by this offence. The defendants entered RAF Fairford with an intent to damage aircraft. They argued that preparing weapons for an aggressive war in Iraq was not a lawful activity under international law. The House of Lords ruled that under UK law it was lawful and therefore the defendants had no defence.

Most public order offences require violence or the threat of violence, but the control powers do not. **Figure 6.2** might help you to remember this.

Violence required	Violence not required
Riot	**Public procession**
Violent disorder	**Public assembly**
Affray	**Harassment, alarm or distress**
Fear and provocation of violence	**Trespassory assembly**
Breach of the peace	**Rave**
	Aggravated trespass
	Obstruction of the highway

Figure 6.2: Public order law and violence

Summary: public order offences	
WHAT are public order offences?	Offences designed to deal with public order problems.
WHEN are they used?	The police have a discretion when to use these powers.

■ KEY POINT CHECKLIST

This chapter has covered the following key knowledge points. You can use these to structure your revision, making sure to recall the key details for each point, as covered in this chapter.

- Public processions can be controlled by the police and banned by the home secretary.

- Public assemblies can be controlled by the police.
- Trespassory assemblies and raves can be banned and dispersed.
- Breach of the peace is violence or threats of violence. It is the duty of the police to prevent it.
- Riot, violent disorder and affray are offences involving violence or the threat of violence.
- Fear or provocation of violence involves insulting, abusive or threatening words.
- Causing harassment, alarm or distress involves insulting, abusive or threatening words.
- Aggravated trespass is trespass that disrupts lawful activity.

■ KEY TERMS AND CONCEPTS

- breach of the peace (**page 100**)
- binding over (**page 102**)

■ SQE1-STYLE QUESTIONS

QUESTION 1

The police learn that a man plans to lead a public procession through the streets of a major town to protest police violence. He has not notified the police of the procession.

Which of the following best summarises the legal position?

A. The failure to notify means that the police may ban the public procession.

B. The failure to notify means that the police may ban the public procession with the permission of the home secretary.

C. The failure to notify means that the police may ban the public procession with the permission of the local council and home secretary.

D. The failure to notify means that the police may impose conditions on the route of the procession.

E. The failure to notify means that the police may prosecute the man for an offence.

QUESTION 2

A man is a supporter of United and attends a football match against City. When he leaves the ground, he and his fellow United supporters are stopped from walking to the railway station by the police. In the previous fixture between United and City there had been many violent clashes between the supporters of the two clubs. The police tell the United supporters that they must wait one hour for the City supporters to disperse. The man refuses to obey the police officer, tries to push past him and is arrested.

Which of the following best summarises the legal position?

A. The police have no power to deprive the man of his liberty. ⌃

B. The police may arrest for breach of the peace.

C. The police may arrest for obstruction of the highway. ✗

D. The police may arrest because this is an unauthorised public procession. ✗

E. The police may arrest because this is an unauthorised public assembly.

QUESTION 3

Two men are drunk when they leave a public house and begin fighting. A barmaid leaving work sees them, is frightened and calls the police. A police officer arrests both men.

Which of the following offences have the two men committed?

A. Riot.

B. Violent disorder.

C. Affray.

D. Fear or provocation of violence.

E. Harassment, alarm or distress.

QUESTION 4

A man invites a group of friends to his house for a party that will last several days with music being played. These parties are frequent and have been very noisy in the past, disturbing the man's neighbours. The neighbours ask the local chief officer of police to stop the party.

Which of the following best summarises the legal position?

A. The chief officer can stop the party because it is a breach of the peace.

B. The chief officer can stop the party because it is trespassory assembly.

C. The chief officer can stop the party because it is a rave.

D. The chief officer can arrest for causing harassment, alarm or distress.

E. The chief officer can stop the party because it is an unauthorised public assembly.

QUESTION 5

A large crowd of people, who support animal rights, gather on the pavement outside a shop selling animals. They display signs and shout slogans indicating their disapproval of this trade, but do not use or threaten any violence or make any insulting remarks. Many passers-by stop to watch, and the street is completely blocked to people and vehicles. The police ask the protesters to disperse and when they refuse, arrest them.

Which of the following crimes have the protesters committed?

A. Obstruction of the highway.

B. Aggravated trespass.

C. Causing harassment, alarm or distress.

D. Fear or provocation of violence.

E. Breach of the peace.

■ ANSWERS TO QUESTIONS

Answers to 'What do you know already?' questions at the start of the chapter

1) The correct answer was (a), (b) and (c). The POA 1986 requires all three to agree.

2) The correct answer was (a). The POA 1986 requires two people.

3) The correct answer was (b). Breach of the peace requires violence or the threat of violence.

4) True. Breach of the peace is a preventative power and unless a person resists a police officer there is no offence.

5) Riot carries the heaviest sentence.

6) The correct answer was (b).

Answers to end-of-chapter SQE1-style questions

Question 1:

The correct answer was E. This is because the power to ban the procession or impose conditions depends upon the senior officer of police reasonably believing that the procession may result in serious public disorder, serious damage to property or serious disruption to the life of the community or that the purpose of the organisers is to intimidate others. Failure to notify is just an offence that may be committed by the organiser.

Question 2:

The correct answer was B. This is because the previous violence makes it reasonable to believe that violence might recur. The police may take reasonable steps to prevent this happening. This includes temporarily detaining people and if they refuse, arresting them.

Question 3:

The correct answer was C. This is because 12 persons are required for riot, 3 for violent disorder and we are not told that either party has used threatening, abusive or insulting words. Two persons fighting could be an affray and the barmaid is a person of reasonable firmness, who might fear for her safety.

Question 4:

The correct answer was D. This is because breach of the peace is violence, not noise. It is not a trespassory assembly or a rave, because the partygoers are not trespassers. Public assemblies do not have to be authorised. Harassment, alarm or distress can be committed by the disorderly conduct of those inside a building, causing distress to those outside.

Question 5:

The correct answer was A. A small demonstration on the highway may be permitted, but blocking the highway is not allowed. They are not trespassing nor using violence or threatening words.

■ KEY CASES, RULES, STATUTES AND INSTRUMENTS

The SQE1 Assessment Specification does not require you to remember the names of the following two cases, but they both contain important principles that are worth remembering:

• *Austin v Commissioner of Police for the Metropolis* [2009] UKHL 5 – police powers to prevent a breach of the peace.
• *DPP v Jones (Margaret) and Another* [1999] 2 AC 240 – there is a right to protest.

7

Judicial review

■ MAKE SURE YOU KNOW

This chapter will cover the main aspects of the nature, process and limits of judicial review, its supervisory nature, the remedies available, the decisions that may be challenged, standing, time limits and the grounds of challenge (illegality, irrationality, procedural impropriety and legitimate expectation) that you will need to know and be able to apply to scenarios, problems and situations for your SQE1 assessment.

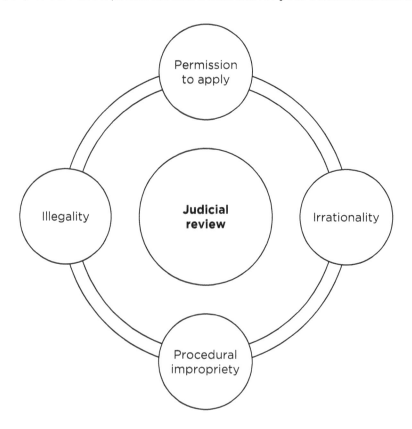

■ SQE ASSESSMENT ADVICE

As you work through this chapter, remember to pay particular attention in your revision to:
• the procedure to apply for judicial review
• the grounds for judicial review
• illegality
• irrationality
• procedural impropriety
• legitimate expectation.

■ WHAT DO YOU KNOW ALREADY?

Have a go at these questions before reading this chapter. If you find some difficult or cannot remember the answers, make a note to look more closely at that subtopic during your revision.

1) Judicial review is an appeal from a decision. True or false?
   [Application for judicial review, page 114]

2) Judicial review is available against:
   a) any person
   b) a government body   *Public Function*
   c) any person or body exercising a public function.
   [Public body, page 116]

3) A claimant for judicial review must have been affected financially by the decision about which they complain. True or false?
   [Sufficient interest, page 115]

4) Illegality is one of the grounds for judicial review. It means that:
   a) the decision maker has committed a crime
   b) the decision maker has broken the law
   c) the decision maker has misinterpreted their legal powers.
   [Illegality, page 120]

5) Irrationality is one of the grounds of judicial review. It means that:
   a) the judge disagrees with the decision
   b) a reasonable man disagrees with the decision
   c) no sensible person could have made the decision.
   [Irrationality, page 123]

6) Natural justice means that:
   a) there should be no discrimination
   b) there is a right to a fair hearing
   c) there should be equal access to justice. *rule of law.*
   [Procedural impropriety, page 124]

INTRODUCTION TO JUDICIAL REVIEW

Judicial review is a process by which the courts (the judiciary) control the decisions and actions of the government (the executive - see **Chapter 1, Separation of powers, page 12**). The courts ensure that the government is acting legally, within the powers granted by an Act of Parliament or the royal prerogative (see **Chapter 4, page 68**). If the government is acting outside those powers the decision is **ultra vires** and it is therefore something that the government cannot do.

Key term: ultra vires

Latin for 'beyond one's powers'.

APPLICATION FOR JUDICIAL REVIEW

In this section you will be able to revise what you need to know for SQE1 about applying for judicial review, including:

- leave - permission to proceed
- **sufficient interest** - the claimant's rights are affected
- **public body** - only public bodies can be judicially reviewed
- excluding judicial review - Acts of Parliament may attempt to prevent judicial review
- remedies.

In a judicial review, the court does not look at the merits of the decision or whether the court considers that it was the right decision, but at the process by which it was made. In that way, judicial review differs from an appeal, in which the merits of the decision may be reconsidered.

The procedure for judicial review is laid down by s 31 of the Senior Courts Act 1981 and part 54 of the Civil Procedure Rules. The claimant applies to the Administrative Court, which is part of the High Court, to 'review the lawfulness of a decision, action or failure to act in relation to the exercise of a public function'.

Exam warning

Revising procedural rules might seem dull, but remember that SQE1 is an exam with a practical focus and you might well be asked about the procedure to apply for judicial review.

Leave - permission to proceed

Unlike other court actions, the claimant must first seek permission to apply for judicial review. This is usually decided by a court official looking at the claim form, which will state the grounds, the remedy sought and the facts relied upon. If permission is refused, the claimant may request an oral hearing.

Permission will be granted if:
• the claim is arguable and it has a reasonable prospect of success
• the claim form is filed not later than three months after the grounds to make the claim first arose – the time limit for planning decisions is six weeks and these time limits are strictly applied.

Permission will be refused if:
• there is a suitable alternative remedy, such as a statutory appeal or an internal appeal
• it is highly likely that the outcome for the applicant would not have been substantially different if the conduct complained of had not occurred, meaning that the public body's decision would have been the same if it had been made lawfully.

Look at **Practice example 7.1** for how this works.

Practice example 7.1

A client has been convicted at the magistrates' court, but he disagrees with his conviction and sentence and seeks a judicial review. Advise him.

As you should know from your other studies, there are statutory rights of appeal from the magistrates' court. There is a rehearing in the Crown Court, or a case can be stated for the divisional court of the High Court. The latter procedure raises a point of law, so it resembles judicial review. It is extremely unlikely that your client would be given leave for judicial review, unless they could show that the magistrates' court had made a serious legal error that could not be corrected in either type of statutory appeal.

Sufficient interest

The claimant must have 'a sufficient interest in the matter to which the application relates'. This means that the decision affected some right or interest of the claimant, such as students expelled from the UK in *Schmidt v Secretary of State for Home Affairs* [1969] 2 Ch 149. Sufficient interest is flexible and is more likely to be granted if the court considers that the claimant has a strong case, or they raise an important issue that needs to be decided. For example, a concerned citizen, Gina Miller, was permitted to bring a judicial review about leaving the European Union (EU) in *R (Miller) v Secretary of State for Exiting the EU* [2017] UKSC 5.

Key term: sufficient interest
Means the right or capacity to bring an action or appear in court. It used to be called *locus standi* or standing.

Interest or pressure groups may seek permission to bring judicial review and, as we can see in **Table 7.1**, the court will look at the same factors when deciding whether the group has sufficient interest.

Public body

Judicial review may only be brought against a body or person exercising a public function. A public body is one that derives its powers from an Act of Parliament or the royal prerogative. It would also include people or bodies that are non-statutory, but perform a government or public function. For example, in *R v City Panel on Takeover and Mergers ex parte Datafin* [1987] QB 815, the Stock Exchange and City of London appointed the members of the panel, which regulated the Stock Exchange. This was a public function. The government had decided that there was no need to create a statutory body because this panel was incorporated into its regulatory system.

Table 7.1: Group applications for judicial review

R v Liverpool Corporation ex parte Liverpool Taxi Fleet Operators' Association [1972] 2 QB 299	The association could apply when the corporation increased the number of taxi licences, as it affected their livelihood.
Inland Revenue Commissioners v National Federation of Self-Employed and Small Businesses [1982] AC 617	The federation complained about the tax assessments of Fleet Street workers. They did not have sufficient interest as these assessments were confidential and solely the concern of the taxpayer and the Inland Revenue.
R v Foreign Secretary ex parte World Development Movement [1995] 1 All ER 611	A respected and well-established pressure group had sufficient interest. They raised a serious legal issue and no one else was able to bring the case.
R v Secretary of State for the Environment ex parte Rose Theatre Trust Company Ltd [1990] 2 WLR 186	A group formed for the sole purpose of bringing this case, about the listing of an historic building, had no standing. A public consultation process provided an alternative remedy.

In contrast, in *R v Disciplinary Committee of the Jockey Club ex parte The Aga Khan* [1993] 1 WLR 90, the body regulating horse racing was not created by statute and had no statutory powers. Nor did it perform any public function because it was not part of any government system of regulation. It could be sued for breach of contract, but not judicially reviewed.

Key term: public body

A public body is a body exercising a public function. This can include non-statutory bodies.

Excluding judicial review

An Act of Parliament might try to prevent any challenge to a decision. The courts will generally not accept this, as it restricts access to justice, so they have interpreted Acts of Parliament in an extremely cunning way to evade such restrictions. The following case is the best-known example of this.

Anisminic v Foreign Compensation Commission [1969] 2 AC 147
The Foreign Compensation Act 1950 stated that a 'determination' by the Foreign Compensation Commission (FCC) of any application made to them 'shall not be called in question in any court of law'. If the 'determination' of the FCC was ultra vires it was not valid. The wording of the Act only prevented the court reviewing a 'determination', it did not say that the court could not review a purported or incorrect determination.

Have a look at **Figure 7.1** to revise the main points of applying for judicial review.

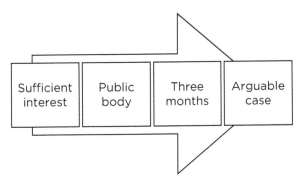

| Sufficient interest | Public body | Three months | Arguable case |

Figure 7.1: Application for judicial review

Table 7.2: Remedies for judicial review

Quashing order	The court rules that the decision of the public body is of no effect and instructs that body to take the decision again, this time legally. The court might substitute its own decision.
Prohibiting order	The court orders the public body not to make or implement an illegal decision.
Mandatory order	The court orders the public body to fulfil its legal duties.
Injunctions	An order to do something or not to do something. An injunction can be interim (interlocutory) and issued to preserve the position before the full trial.
Declarations	The court states the legal position. Public bodies would comply.
Damages	Damages or other forms of compensation are not awarded for judicial review. Damages could only be given if there was also a successful civil case, say in contract or tort, as part of the review.

Remedies

Even if the claimant proves that a decision or action was ultra vires, the court has a discretion whether to grant a remedy. The court might refuse if the claimant has acted unreasonably, a remedy would now be ineffective or it is not in the public interest. There are several remedies available, which can be seen in **Table 7.2.**

Summary: application for judicial review	
WHAT is judicial review?	The court checks the legality of a decision.
WHEN is it used?	Against a person or body exercising a public function.

THE GROUNDS OF JUDICIAL REVIEW

This section gives you a quick overview of the main grounds for judicial review that you need to know for SQE1. These grounds are conveniently summarised by Lord Diplock in *Council for Civil Service*

Unions v Minister of State for Civil Service [1985] AC 374 and can be seen in **Table 7.3**.

Table 7.3: The grounds of judicial review

Illegality	The decision maker must correctly understand the law that regulates his decision-making power and give effect to it.
Irrationality	A decision that is so outrageous in its defiance of logic or of accepted moral standards that no sensible person who had applied his mind to the question to be decided could have arrived at it.
Procedural impropriety	A failure to follow procedural rules laid down in legislation or not following the basic rules of **natural justice**.
Proportionality	The decision of the public body may only restrict rights to the minimum necessary to achieve a legitimate objective.

Lord Diplock thought that proportionality would eventually become part of judicial review, but it is only used in European Convention on Human Rights (ECHR) and EU law cases (see **Chapter 8, page 145**).

Revision tip

Lord Diplock's categories are a convenient way for revising judicial review, but a judge might hold that a decision is ultra vires on several different grounds (eg it is both illegal and irrational). There are also many subcategories, or a judge may give reasons that do not seem to easily fit into any of the categories. Look at the cases in this chapter and try to understand the sort of things to which judges object.

Summary: the grounds of judicial review

WHAT are the main grounds of judicial review?	Illegality Irrationality Procedural impropriety

ILLEGALITY

This section enables you to revise the different types of illegality:
- misunderstanding the law
- improper purpose
- relevant and irrelevant considerations
- fettering of discretion
- unauthorised delegation
- error of fact.

Misunderstanding the law

Judicial review might be regarded as advanced statutory interpretation. The court will look closely at the wording of the whole Act of Parliament to decide what decisions are allowed. They will look at the policy and objectives of the Act. In *Padfield v Minister of Agriculture* [1968] AC 997, the minister had the power to regulate the price of milk in different regions of the country. He could establish a committee to investigate disparities in the price of milk 'if the minister in any case so directs'. The words seem to give the minister absolute discretion, but the court held that he could not ignore differences in price between regions and issued a mandatory order for him to constitute a committee.

Similarly, in *R v Foreign Secretary ex parte World Development Movement* [1995] 1 All ER 611, the foreign secretary had power to give money to promote the development and *economy* of a country. It was illegal for him to finance a dam, where evidence indicated that it was economically unsound.

The statute must also be interpreted in the context of the general principles of the constitution. In *R (Unison) v Lord Chancellor* [2017] UKSC 51, the legislation seemed to give the Lord Chancellor a general power to set court fees, but this did not allow him to require excessively high fees, because access to the courts was a basic right required by the rule of law (see **Chapter 1, page 12**).

Improper purpose

A statutory power must not be used for a purpose for which it was not intended. For example, in *Porter v Magill* [2002] 2 AC 357, the council had the legal power to sell council houses, but could not use this power to encourage buyers to vote for them.

See **Practice example 7.2** for an illustration of illegal use of a statutory power.

Practice example 7.2

A teacher is dismissed for constantly being late for work. The head teacher, who has always disliked her, refers her case to the Teaching Regulation Agency, who ban her from teaching. The agency has the power to do this for unacceptable professional conduct or conduct that may bring the profession into disrepute. Has the agency acted legally?

No. The court would look closely at the powers of the agency and would conclude that the teacher's behaviour was not serious enough to be unacceptable or disreputable. The head teacher's prejudice might also be an example of improper purpose.

Relevant and irrelevant considerations

The decision maker must only consider relevant matters and not be misled by irrelevant matters. In *R v Somerset County Council ex parte Fewings* [1995] EWCA Civ 24, the council had the power to manage their land for its benefit, improvement or development. This did not allow them to ban stag hunting on their land, to which they had a moral objection.

In *Wheeler v Leicester City Council* [1985] AC 1054, the council banned Leicester rugby club from using a council playing field, because they disapproved of its tour of South Africa. The management of open spaces did not permit the council to ban the club for political reasons.

Fettering of discretion

A public body may adopt a general policy for taking decisions, but it must not stick to the policy rigidly and fail to properly consider individual cases. For example, in *R v Secretary of State for the Home Department ex parte Simms* [2000] 2 AC 115, the home secretary's policy of never allowing journalists to visit prisoners was illegal. It was legitimate for journalists to investigate alleged miscarriages of justice.

Unauthorised delegation

If legislation clearly entrusts a decision to a specified public body, that body cannot allow someone else to take that decision. In *Lavender v Minister of Housing and Local Government* [1970] 1 WLR 1231, the minister of housing rejected a planning application because the minister of agriculture objected to it. The rejection was void.

Error of fact

Normally the decision maker is entitled to decide disputed facts, but a decision cannot be based on facts that are incorrect, are relevant to the decision and cause unfairness. For example, in *R v Criminal Injuries Compensation Board ex parte A* [1999] 2 AC 330, the board did not see a vital doctor's report when assessing compensation.

Look at **Figure 7.2** to quickly revise the different types of illegality.

Figure 7.2: Illegality

Summary: illegality	
WHAT is illegality?	A decision maker misunderstands or misapplies their legal powers.
HOW does a court decide what is illegal?	By closely examining the statutory power.
WHAT are the consequences of illegality?	The decision is void and has no effect.

IRRATIONALITY

This section enables you to revise how irrationality is defined by the courts:

• Wednesbury unreasonableness
• human rights
• what is unreasonable.

Wednesbury unreasonableness

This is a decision that is so perverse or absurd that it cannot be allowed to stand. It is sometimes called 'Wednesbury unreasonableness', because it was defined in *Associated Provincial Picture Houses v Wednesbury Corporation* [1948] 1 KB 223. Wednesbury had the power to license cinemas and required that children under 15 should not be admitted on Sundays. Lord Greene MR stated that he could overrule 'a conclusion so unreasonable that no reasonable authority could have come to it.'

This case is the accepted definition of Wednesbury unreasonableness, but, on the facts, the court did not think Wednesbury's decision was unreasonable. At that time religious observance on Sunday was more common.

Human rights

In human rights cases, the court will investigate reasonableness more closely, but it is still difficult to prove that a decision is irrational, as shown in *R v Ministry of Defence ex parte Smith* [1996] QB 517. The ministry's policy was that homosexuality was incompatible with service in the armed forces. Although the judges personally disagreed, they did not think that it was irrational. It was not beyond the range of responses available to a reasonable decision maker. The ministry's decision did not outrageously defy logic.

What is unreasonable

In *Roberts v Hopwood* [1925] AC 528, Poplar Council adopted a policy of paying a wage of £4 a week to all its employees, male and female. This was unreasonable. The average wage was £2.50 a week and falling. It was a socialist policy at the expense of the ratepayers.

Unreasonableness is hard to prove, as can be seen in **Practice example 7.3**.

Practice example 7.3

The local council has used its statutory power of investment to buy a shopping centre for £50 million. Many other councils had made similar purchases and the council took professional advice. A local council taxpayer thinks that this is an unwise and risky use of public money. Advise the council taxpayer.

We are told that the council has the legal power to do this, so the council taxpayer would have to show that this was an irrational or unreasonable decision. That would be difficult, particularly as the council were just doing as other councils had done. It is not a perverse or absurd decision.

Summary: irrationality

WHAT is irrationality?	A decision so absurd that no sensible person could have reached it.
WHEN is it used?	Not very often. It is hard to prove that a government decision is not just wrong, but irrational.

PROCEDURAL IMPROPRIETY

This section will enable you to revise procedural impropriety:
• the requirement to consult
• natural justice
• legitimate expectation.

The requirement to consult

An Act of Parliament may lay down a procedure to be followed, such as the serving of notices or the consultation of interested parties, before a decision is taken or delegated legislation is enacted. The court will decide whether the procedure is mandatory (one that must be followed) or directory (optional). That will depend upon how important the consequences of failing to follow the procedure are. In **Table 7.4** we can see two examples where failure to consult was unlawful.

Table 7.4: Consultation

Bradbury v Enfield LBC [1967] 1 WLR 1311	Enfield had to give public notice of proposals to close schools so that interested parties could comment. They planned to close eight schools and failed to do this.
	Lord Denning ordered Enfield to give notice.
Agricultural, Horticultural and Forestry Training Board v Aylesbury Mushrooms [1972] 1 WLR 190	The minister had to consult before he made regulations. He could not just consult the National Farmers' Union but must consult all the organisations affected.

Natural justice

Natural justice is the right to a fair hearing and applies when a decision of a public body affects the rights of an individual. It applied when the chief constable of Brighton was dismissed from office in *Ridge v Baldwin* [1964] AC 40 and when the council knocked down a man's house without consulting him in *Cooper v Wandsworth Board of Works* (1863) 14 CB (NS) 180. What is a fair hearing depends upon the body taking the decision, the questions that need to be decided and the consequences of the decision for the claimant. There are two basic principles of natural justice: the rule against bias and the right to a fair hearing.

Key term: natural justice

Natural justice is a legal concept with two main elements: the rules against bias and the right to a fair hearing.

The rule against bias

A person should not take a decision if they have a personal interest in the outcome. It is not necessary to prove that the decision maker was actually biased, merely that it is the impression they give. The test to decide this comes from *Porter v Magill* [2002] 2 AC 357: 'Whether the fair-minded and informed observer, having considered the facts, would conclude that there was a real possibility that the tribunal was biased'. **Table 7.5** has three examples of this.

Table 7.5: Examples of apparent bias

Ridge v Baldwin [1964] AC 40	The council dismissed the chief constable based on newspaper reports of a trial. They had already decided he was unsuitable and so were incapable of giving him a fair hearing.
Dimes v Grand Junction Canal Co (1852) 3 HLC 759	Lord Chancellor Cottenham decided this case. He was a substantial shareholder in the company, so his decision was quashed.
R v Bow Street Magistrate ex parte Pinochet [2000] 1 AC 119	Lord Hoffman, a member of Amnesty International, sat on a human rights case, where Amnesty International gave evidence to the court. The case had to be heard again, without Lord Hoffman.

The right to a fair hearing

The accused person must be given the opportunity to put their side of the case. What amounts to a fair hearing very much depends upon the circumstances, but the minimum would be that the person should be told what they are accused of and allowed to respond before the decision is taken: *Ridge v Baldwin* [1964] AC 40. As can be seen in **Table 7.6**, the more serious the consequences of the decision, the more rights the claimant has.

Table 7.6: Examples of a fair hearing

Lloyds v McMahon [1987] AC 625	The claimants were only entitled to a written hearing because they knew the charge against them and had the right of appeal to the High Court anyway.
Osborn v Parole Board [2013] UKSC 61	The Parole Board should have offered the applicants oral hearings. The liberty of the prisoners was at stake. Important facts were in dispute, so witnesses needed to be questioned to establish the truth of those facts.
R (G) v Governors of X School [2012] 1 AC 167	Allowing the claimant legal representation is appropriate when they could be banned from teaching.
R v Secretary of State for the Home Department ex parte Doody [1994] 1 AC 531	Fairness required that life prisoners should be told the reasons for their minimum period of detention. There is a general duty to give reasons unless there is justification for not doing so.

Look at **Practice example 7.4** for how natural justice works.

Practice example 7.4

The Southtown Archaeology Club allows any member of the public to join. The club is conducting an excavation in Southtown and are told that a member, Joanna, has stolen jewellery discovered in the dig. The chair of the club sends Joanna a text message cancelling her membership. No reason is given, nor is Joanna given any chance to explain. Can Joanna seek judicial review?

No. By any standards her treatment is unfair and none of the basic standards of natural justice have been met. The catch is that, although the club is open to the public, it is not a public body, nor is it carrying out any public functions. Depending upon the rules of the club, she might be able to sue for breach of contract, but not judicial review.

You can quickly revise the main points of natural justice by looking at **Figure 7.3**.

Legitimate expectation

There are two types of legitimate expectation: procedural legitimate expectation and substantive legitimate expectation.

Procedural legitimate expectation

As part of natural justice, a claimant may have a legitimate expectation that they will be consulted about a change in the rules or a decision that will affect them. This can be seen in *Council for Civil Service Unions v Minister of State for Civil Service* [1985], where the minister proposed to ban trade union membership. The council had a legitimate expectation that they would be consulted, as they had been in the past about changes to terms and conditions.

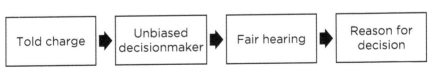

Figure 7.3: Natural justice

Substantive legitimate expectation

Legitimate expectation has been extended so that, in certain circumstances, public bodies may be obliged to keep a promise that they have made about their future policies. In *R v North and East Devon Health Authority ex parte Coughlan* [2001] QB 213, Coughlan and seven other severely disabled patients had been told that they could stay in their National Health Service (NHS) accommodation for life. Later, Devon wanted to close their facility.

The patients had a substantive legitimate expectation and Devon must keep their promise. It would be unfair and an abuse of power to close and Devon could not show that there was an overriding public interest that justified closure.

R (Niazi) v Secretary of State for Home Affairs [2008] EWCA Civ 755 clarifies the rules for substantive legitimate expectation. There must be:
• a clear and unequivocal undertaking
• given to a particular group or individual
• but the defendant could defeat the claim by showing that there was good reason for departing from the undertaking.

Exam warning

The question will not always make clear that it is about judicial review. As you will have seen from this chapter, judicial review covers lots of different areas of law. Look for someone questioning a decision taken by a government body or government official, then think of the main areas of judicial review. Does anyone have sufficient interest and was the decision illegal, irrational or procedurally improper?

■ KEY POINT CHECKLIST

This chapter has covered the following key knowledge points. You can use these to structure your revision, making sure to recall the key details for each point, as covered in this chapter.
• Judicial review does not look at the merits of a decision. It looks at whether the decision was taken legally.
• A person with sufficient interest may apply for judicial review against any person or body exercising a public function.

- Illegality means that the public body has made a decision that it did not have the legal power to make.   Ultra Vires
- Irrationality means that the public body has made a decision that is absurd.
- Procedural impropriety means that the public body has not followed the correct legal procedure.
- Natural justice is the right to a fair hearing.
- A legitimate expectation is a promise that must be kept.

■ KEY TERMS AND CONCEPTS

- ultra vires (**page 114**)
- sufficient interest (**page 116**)
- public body (**page 117**)
- natural justice (**page 125**)

■ SQE1-STYLE QUESTIONS

QUESTION 1

A local council refuse a building firm planning permission to build an estate. The firm appeal, but the planning inspector upholds the refusal. The planning inspector is the brother of the chair of the council. The building firm seek judicial review of the decision to refuse planning permission.

Which of the following arguments would be the most likely to succeed?

A. The refusal is irrational.

B. The refusal is illegal.

C. The refusal is a breach of legitimate expectation.

D. The refusal is a fettering of discretion.

E. The refusal is a breach of natural justice.

QUESTION 2

The secretary of state has power under the [fictitious] Carbon Act 2021 to make regulations on the type of fuel used by airliners, as he sees fit. The Act requires that, before making the regulations, the secretary of state shall consult any employer appearing to him to be a substantial employer of persons engaged in aircraft manufacturing. The secretary of state makes regulations, but does not consult a company that is the largest aircraft manufacturer in the UK.

Which of the following best summarises the legal position?

A. The secretary of state has the power to make any regulations that he wants.

B. The secretary of state has absolute discretion on whom he consults.

C. The secretary of state has a duty to consult the company.

D. The secretary of state may make any regulations he wants, as long as they are neither illegal nor irrational.

E. The secretary of state may not make the regulations without the agreement of the company.

QUESTION 3

A local council decides that all children in its schools should receive free school meals, irrespective of their family income. The council raises the rate of council tax to pay for this.

Which of the following would have sufficient interest to apply for judicial review of the decision?

A. Any legal person.

B. Any incorporated or statutory body.

C. The secretary of state for education.

D. Local council taxpayers.

E. The prime minister.

QUESTION 4

Local councils have the power to grant licences to drive a taxi. A woman applies for a licence but is told by the council that it is not their policy to grant any more taxi licences for their area.

Which of the following would be the woman's best course of action?

A. The woman should apply for judicial review.

B. The woman should sue for breach of contract.

C. The woman should apply to the European Court of Human Rights. ⟵

D. The woman should be advised that the council has the power to refuse licence applications.

E. The woman should sue the council for negligent performance of their duties. ✗

QUESTION 5

The NHS provides a home for seven severely ill patients and has assured them that this accommodation will be available for the rest of their lives. Because of a policy change, the NHS decides to close this home and transfer the seven patients to local council care. The patients object to this change and apply for judicial review.

Which of the following best summarises the legal position?

A. The patients do not have sufficient interest.

B. The NHS may move the patients if it is in the public interest. ✓

C. The NHS has no obligation to consult the patients. ✗

D. The NHS has no legal power to make this decision. ✗

E. The NHS is not a public body. ✗

■ ANSWERS TO QUESTIONS

Answers to 'What do you know already?' questions at the start of the chapter

1) False. Judicial review is not a rehearing and does not look at the merits of a decision. It just checks whether the decision was taken legally.

2) The correct answer was (c). Usually it is government bodies that are judicially reviewed, but it is possible for a private body or person to exercise a public function. ✓

3) False. The claimant must have sufficient interest, which means that the decision affects them in some significant way. It does not have to be financial.

4) The correct answer was (c). Illegality means that the decision maker has misunderstood or misapplied their powers.

5) The correct answer was (c). Irrationality does not just mean that a decision is wrong, but so wrong that it is absurd.
6) The correct answer was (b). Natural justice sounds like a vague phrase, but in law it has a very specific meaning.

Answers to end-of-chapter SQE1-style questions

Question 1:

The correct answer was E. The chair of the council is related to the planning inspector. This would give the appearance of bias to the fair-minded and informed observer. There is no need to prove that there was actual bias, just a real possibility of it.

Question 2:

The correct answer was C. This is because although the secretary of state has discretion upon whom he consults, he must exercise it in a reasonable way. He cannot ignore the largest employer.

Question 3:

The correct answer was D. This is because the local taxpayers are directly affected by the decision, because they must pay more council tax. None of the other candidates are affected by the decision.

Question 4:

The correct answer was A. This is because the refusal to grant any licences is a fettering of discretion, which makes the decision illegal. Judicial review is the correct procedure to raise this issue.

Question 5:

The correct answer was B. This is because, although the NHS have made a promise to a small group of people, they will not have raised a substantive legitimate expectation, if the NHS can show that they had sound policy reasons for making the decision and this is not unfair to the claimants.

■ KEY CASES, RULES, STATUTES AND INSTRUMENTS

The SQE1 Assessment Specification does not require you to remember case names. There are a lot of case law examples in this chapter, but do not worry about the names, concentrate on the principles. Here are the most important:

• *R v Foreign Secretary ex parte World Development Movement* [1995] 1 All ER 611 – sufficient interest is a flexible test.

- *R v City Panel on Takeover and Mergers ex parte Datafin* [1987] QB 815 – a private body may perform a public function.
- *Council for Civil Service Unions v Minister of State for Civil Service* [1985] AC 374 – the basic grounds for judicial review.
- *Associated Provincial Picture Houses v Wednesbury Corporation* [1948] 1 KB 223 – the definition of unreasonable.
- *Ridge v Baldwin* [1964] AC 40 – the basic requirements of natural justice.

8

Human rights

■ MAKE SURE YOU KNOW

This chapter will cover the main aspects of the Human Rights Act 1998 and the European Convention on Human Rights (ECHR), in particular ss 2, 3, 4, 6, 7, 8 and 10 of the Human Rights Act and Schedule 1 of the Act, which contains the 'convention rights'. You will need to know about these topics and be able to apply them to scenarios, problems and situations for your SQE1 assessment.

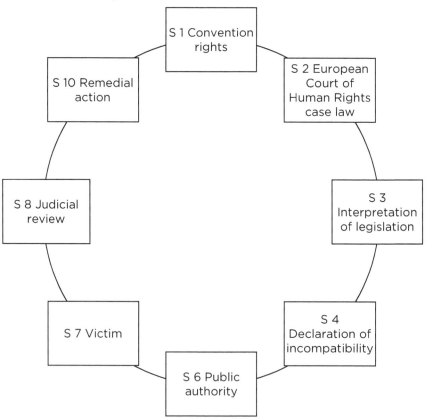

■ SQE ASSESSMENT ADVICE

As you work through this chapter, remember to pay particular attention in your revision to:
• the Human Rights Act 1998
• convention rights.

■ WHAT DO YOU KNOW ALREADY?

Have a go at these questions before reading this chapter. If you find some difficult or cannot remember the answers, make a note to look more closely at that subtopic during your revision.

1) The Human Rights Act 1998 created new rights for the UK. True or false?
   [The Council of Europe, page 136]

2) A UK court or tribunal:
   a) must take into account decisions by the European Court of Human Rights
   b) is bound by decisions of the European Court of Human Rights
   c) makes its own decisions on the meaning of the European Court of Human Rights.
   [Interpretation of convention rights, page 137]

3) Which of the following can a UK court or tribunal *not* do?
   a) declare an Act of Parliament incompatible with the ECHR.
   b) interpret an Act of Parliament so that it is compatible with the ECHR
   c) declare an Act of Parliament void because it is incompatible with the ECHR.
   [Interpretation of legislation, page 137; declarations of incompatibility, page 138]

4) Which of the following may bring proceedings under the Human Rights Act 1998?
   a) a victim
   b) a public authority
   c) a pressure group.
   [Proceedings and judicial remedies, page 140]

5) Since the Human Rights Act 1998 came into force it is no longer possible for a claimant to apply to the European Court of Human Rights. True or false?
   [The European Court of Human Rights, page 146]

THE COUNCIL OF EUROPE

The Council of Europe is an organisation that came into existence in 1949 to promote human rights, democracy and the rule of law. Inspired by the United Nations Universal Declaration on Human Rights of 1948, the council drafted its own ECHR in 1950, which came into force in 1953. Under this treaty, European states, including the UK, undertook to respect the rights guaranteed in the convention. The convention set up the European Court of Human Rights to enforce and define the meaning of the rights protected. It is *important to note* that the Council of Europe is a separate organisation from the European Union (EU), so the Human Rights Act 1998 is unaffected by the UK's withdrawal from the EU.

Exam warning

EU law works differently to the European Court of Human Rights. Unlike the EU, the Council of Europe has no power to legislate for its member states. The rights in the convention do not have supremacy over UK law. Under EU law there was a direct link requiring UK courts to refer cases to the Court of Justice of the EU. There is no such link to the European Court of Human Rights for cases involving convention rights.

THE HUMAN RIGHTS ACT 1998

The Human Rights Act 1998 was passed to enable persons to enforce their 'convention rights' in UK courts. This section will enable you to revise:

- parliamentary sovereignty and the Human Rights Act
- interpretation of convention rights
- interpretation of legislation
- **declarations of incompatibility**
- **public authorities**
- proceedings and judicial remedies.

Parliamentary sovereignty and the Human Rights Act

The Human Rights Act can be repealed or amended, just like any other Act of Parliament. The Act does not prevent Parliament making laws that infringe human rights. Section 19 provides that, when *new* legislation is proposed, the minister in charge of the Bill must make a 'statement of compatibility' (eg declare that the Bill does not infringe the convention). *Or* state that he/she is unable to make a statement of compatibility, but the government wants to proceed with the Bill.

Interpretation of convention rights

Section 2 requires all UK courts and tribunals to 'take into account' the case law of the European Court of Human Rights, when deciding upon the meaning of a 'convention right'.

This was explained by Lord Slynn in *R (Alconbury Developments Ltd) v Secretary of State for the Environment* [2003] 2 AC 295 at 313: 'In the absence of some special circumstances it seems to me that the court should follow any clear and consistent jurisprudence of the European Court of Human Rights'.

It is thought desirable to maintain a consistent interpretation of the convention if possible. This means that the Supreme Court should follow the case decisions of the European Court of Human Rights unless:
• there is no decision of the European Court of Human Rights on the matter
• there are conflicting decisions of the European Court of Human Rights on the matter
• the previous decision of the European Court of Human Rights was on UK law and failed to properly understand UK law.

If a court below the Supreme Court is confronted with conflicting decisions from the European Court of Human Rights and a higher UK court, the UK court must abide by the normal precedent system and follow the decision of the higher UK court. If the litigants are dissatisfied, their remedy is to appeal to the higher UK court.

Interpretation of legislation

Section 3 states that: 'So far as it is possible to do so, primary legislation and subordinate legislation must be read and given effect in a way which is compatible with the Convention rights'.

This has led the courts to develop a new type of statutory interpretation, where the court might not give the words their literal meaning or might even 'read down' or add extra words to the legislation. This process can be seen in the case of *Ghaidan v Godin-Mendoza* [2004] 2 AC 557. The Rent Act 1977 provided that a surviving spouse or the survivor of a couple who lived together as husband and wife could succeed to a tenancy. The court had to decide whether a cohabiting same-sex couple could be regarded as living together as husband and wife. The House of Lords ruled that Article 8, the right to a family life, would be infringed unless the legislation was interpreted in such a way that the two men were deemed to have lived together as husband and wife. It is worth noting that this case was decided *before* same-sex marriage became legal in 2014.

Revision tip

If the courts cannot interpret the primary legislation to comply with human rights, s 3 makes clear that the primary legislation remains the law. Primary legislation is defined as an Act of Parliament or an Order in Council.

In contrast, subordinate (delegated legislation) could be declared invalid if it contravenes convention rights (see **Chapter 5, page 87**).

Declarations of incompatibility

Section 4 states that if it is not possible to interpret primary legislation, such as an Act of Parliament, so that it is compatible with the convention rights, then the High Court (or above) may make a declaration of incompatibility. The primary legislation remains in force and then it is up to Parliament whether it wants to change the law and remedy the breach of human rights.

Key term: declaration of incompatibility

A court may declare that a law breaches the convention rights protected under the Human Rights Act 1998. However, the court has no power to make that law invalid.

Parliament could repeal or amend the offending legislation using an ordinary Act of Parliament, or s 10 allows a 'fast-track' procedure using delegated legislation (see **Chapter 5, page 87**).

R (Anderson) v Home Secretary [2002] 4 All ER 108 is an early example of a declaration of incompatibility. The home secretary had the statutory power to decide the minimum prison sentence (the tariff) to be served by a life prisoner. The court decided that this was a breach of Article 6, the right to a fair trial. A judge should decide a sentence, not a politician.

Parliament complied with the declaration of incompatibility, changed the law and now the courts decide the tariff.

Revision tip

Most declarations of incompatibility lead to a change in the law, but it is *important to note* that, as Parliament is sovereign, it may decline to change the law.

See **Practice example 8.1** for an illustration of this.

Practice example 8.1

Your client is convinced that an Act of Parliament contravenes her human rights and wants the court to declare the Act unlawful. How would you advise this client?

It is not possible for the court to do this. They might be able to interpret the Act in a way that is compatible with human rights, but if the court cannot do this, they could only make a declaration of incompatibility. Parliament could amend or repeal the Act, but the court cannot order Parliament to do so.

Public authorities

By becoming a party to the European Court of Human Rights, the government has agreed to respect human rights, so the Human Rights Act allows enforcement of those rights against government bodies. Therefore, s 6 states that 'it is unlawful for a public authority to act in a way which is incompatible with a Convention right' and that 'a person is not a public authority ... if the nature of the act is private'.

Key term: public authority

A public authority is defined as 'a court or tribunal' and 'any person certain of whose functions are functions of a public nature'.

The meaning of public authority was considered in *Parishional Church Council of Aston Cantlow v Wallbank* [2003] 3 All ER 1213, which concerned liability to pay for the repair of a church. The court must answer the following questions to decide whether a person or body was a public authority:
• Did the body possess special powers?
• Was there democratic accountability?

- Was there public funding?
- Was there an obligation to only act in the public interest?
- Did the body have a statutory constitution?

The court also said that there could be 'hybrid authorities', which exercised both public and private functions. The public functions could be distinguished by the following characteristics:
- Was there public funding?
- Did the authority have statutory powers?
- Did it take the place of central government or local authorities or provide a public service?

Even if a person was a public or hybrid authority, if they carried out a *private* act, such as repairs to the church, they were not subject to s 6. **Practice example 8.2** shows the distinction between public and private.

Practice example 8.2

A local authority has a statutory duty to house an old lady and pays for her to be accommodated in a privately run care home. The lady is in dispute with the care home and the owners of the home ask her to leave. She claims that her human right to a home under Article 8 ECHR has been infringed. Would Article 8 apply?

The local authority is performing a public function, but the lady would have a contract with the owners, who are not a public authority. Therefore, the Human Rights Act would not apply to the dispute. It would be a contractual dispute between her and the owners of the home.

Courts and tribunals are clearly public authorities under s 6 and so cannot act in a way that is incompatible with human rights. That means that a court must have regard to human rights when deciding upon any area of law. Even in a dispute between two private individuals, human rights could apply. A well-known example is *Campbell v Mirror Group Newspapers* [2004] UKHL 22, where a famous model, Naomi Campbell, was suing a newspaper for taking unauthorised photographs. The House of Lords allowed her to enforce Article 8, the right of privacy, against the newspaper.

Proceedings and judicial remedies

Section 7 requires that only a '**victim** of the unlawful act' may bring or defend proceedings against a 'public authority'. The procedure often adopted is judicial review, which must be brought within one year. To have sufficient interest the claimant must be a victim. 'Victim' means that the claimant must be personally affected by the unlawful act. That could include the family of the victim if the breach of human rights also affected them. Pressure or interest groups cannot apply as it is unlikely that the breach would personally affect them. For example, in *In the Matter of an Application by the Northern Ireland Human Rights Commission for Judicial Review* [2015] UKSC 42, the commission could not complain about abortion law, because it was not personally affected by that law.

Key term: victim

A person (natural or legal) personally affected by a violation of their convention rights.

Section 8 makes available the full range of legal remedies. Damages may be awarded and, in determining the level of compensation, UK courts must 'take account of the principles applied by the European Court of Human Rights'. If damages are awarded, they would be modest and only compensate for physical or financial damage or lost opportunity. The European Court of Human Rights favours 'just satisfaction', an order that the breach of human rights should be corrected. For example, in *R (Greenfield) v Home Secretary* [2005] 1 All ER 927, Greenfield was not given a fair hearing when he was subjected to prison discipline. The court ordered the prison to hold a fair hearing, but awarded no compensation.

Practice example 8.3 provides an illustration of this.

Practice example 8.3

A client seeks your advice about a human rights claim, but only wants to take a case to court if he has a chance of winning large damages. How would you advise this client?

With caution. Even if the client wins, it is likely that they will only receive a court ruling that acknowledges the breach of rights and asks the public authority to remedy it. Punitive or aggravated damages are not awarded, so damages, if any, are likely to be modest.

Judicial review for human rights is different from standard judicial review (**see Chapter 7, page 114**). The definition of sufficient interest is stricter, but the time limit for application is longer and damages are a possibility (**Figure 8.1**).

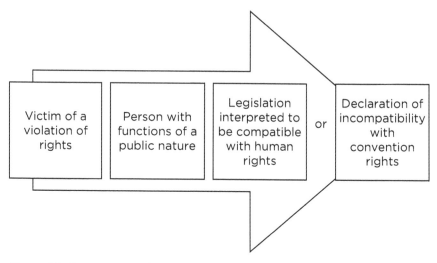

Figure 8.1: Court process for human rights claim

Summary: the Human Rights Act 1998

WHAT is the Human Rights Act 1998?	An Act that allows the ECHR to be enforced in UK courts.
WHO is it enforced against?	Public authorities.
WHO is it used by?	Victims of a violation of rights.

CONVENTION RIGHTS

This section will enable you to revise:
• rights under the ECHR
• interpretation of convention rights
• the European Court of Human Rights.

Under the convention the UK is obliged to secure the convention rights to everyone within its jurisdiction. This would usually mean the territory of the UK, but, in exceptional circumstances the rights apply outside the UK. In the early part of this century, the UK was the occupying power in part of Iraq. The European Court of Human Rights ruled in *Al Skeini v UK* (2011) 53 EHRR 13 that the UK had jurisdiction because they exercised authority and control over the people in that area. Under the same logic, the convention applies to UK military personnel when serving outside the UK: *Smith v Ministry of Defence* [2013] UKSC 41.

Rights under the ECHR

SQE1 requires you to know about the convention rights. **Table 8.1** helps remind you of these rights and their main features.

Table 8.1: Convention rights in schedule 1 of the Human Rights Act 1998

The rights protected	Summary of the right
Article 2 Right to life	No one shall be deprived of his life, but deprivation of life is permitted in self-defence.
	Deaths in prison and other suspicious deaths must be properly investigated at an inquest.
Article 3 Prohibition of torture	Torture or inhuman or degrading treatment are prohibited.
	Evidence obtained by torture outside the UK cannot be admitted in court.
	To deport someone to harsh conditions is inhuman or degrading and contrary to Article 3.
Article 4 Prohibition of slavery and forced labour	No one shall be held in slavery or servitude.
	Slavery is illegal in the UK but forced labour still occurs. The Modern Slavery Act 2015 applies.
Article 5 Right to liberty and security	No one should be deprived of their liberty without a trial.
	An arrested person must be told the reason for their arrest.
Article 6 Right to a fair trial	Civil rights and obligations and criminal charges must be determined by a fair and public hearing.
	Access to legal advice must be permitted.
Article 7 No punishment without law	It is not a crime if it was not against the law when the act was committed.
Article 8 Right to respect for private and family life, home and correspondence.	Deportation might infringe the right to family life.
	Civil partnerships must be extended to opposite-sex couples.
	Discrimination against homosexuals is not permitted.
	Privacy and personal data are protected.
Article 9 Freedom of thought, conscience and religion	Any religion is permitted, but manifesting that religion may be restricted if it infringes the rights and freedoms of others.

Convention rights ... (continued)

The rights protected	Summary of the right
Article 10 Freedom of expression	The right to hold or communicate opinions, information or ideas.
	This right may be restricted to protect national security, prevent crime, protect morals or to protect the Article 8 privacy rights of others.
Article 11 Freedom of assembly and association	Political parties and other associations may be made illegal to protect national security, prevent crime, protect morals or the protect the rights of others.
Article 12 Right to marry	Men and women have the right to marry and found a family. There are no restrictions on this right, but there can be national laws governing marriage.
Article 14 Prohibition of discrimination	No discrimination is permitted in the enjoyment of convention rights.
Protocol 1 Article 1 Protection of property	Every person is entitled to the peaceful enjoyment of their possessions, but they can be deprived of them in the public interest.
Protocol 1 Article 2 Right to education	Everyone has a right to education.
	The religious and philosophical convictions of parents must be respected.
Protocol 1 Article 3 Right to free elections	Free elections, at reasonable intervals by secret ballot.
	A ban on all prisoners voting is not permitted.
Protocol 13 Abolition of the death penalty	The death penalty is prohibited, except in time of war.

Revision tip

Remembering all these rights might seem like a big task, but most of them are the sort of rights that you would expect to exist in a country like the UK, and you do not have to remember the Article numbers.

Interpretation of convention rights

Most of the rights in the ECHR have some qualifications or exceptions, which allow the right to be restricted.

Restrictions on rights

The only unqualified right is Article 3. Torture or inhuman or degrading treatment are never permitted. All the other rights have exceptions. Articles 8 to 11 have a long list of exceptions. We shall take Article 8.2, the right to a private life, as a typical example to explain how the exceptions work: 'There shall be no interference by a public authority with the exercise of this right except such as is in accordance with the law and is necessary in a democratic society in the interests of national security, public safety or the economic well-being of the country, for the prevention of disorder or crime, for the protection of health or morals, or for the protection of the rights and freedoms of others'.

The right is the important thing, and the public authority must justify why they are interfering with it. The restrictions must be clearly specified by the law and understandable to people. Either the restriction of the human right must be authorised by a judge in advance (a search warrant would be an example), or it should be possible to complain to the courts about the infringement of rights.

The concept of **proportionality** is used to decide whether restricting a right is acceptable. The court will decide whether there is a legitimate aim in restricting the right, which would usually be one of the exceptions, as in our **Practice example 8.2**, and whether
• the restriction would achieve that aim
• whether a less intrusive restriction could be used
• whether there is a fair balance between the right and the community need to restrict it.

Key term: proportionality

The restriction of a right should be no more than is necessary to protect the public interest.

Let us look at some examples. A convicted terrorist, who was not a British citizen, could be deported, which would interfere with their family life, to protect national security or public safety. The government would have to show that there was no realistic alternative and the court would assess the effect on the terrorist's family. Convicted foreign criminals could also be deported to prevent disorder or crime, but the court would have to decide whether there was fair balance between the rights of the individual and the public interest. Personal privacy is protected, unless there is a more pressing need to expose crime or immoral behaviour, such as public figures lying to the public. A person's home could be compulsorily purchased if there was an economic need to build a motorway or railway line. The police may keep data on individuals to prevent crime, but would have to show that the data was only used for that purpose and only kept on those who were actually a threat.

The European Court of Human Rights

A victim may bring a complaint, against the UK, to the European Court of Human Rights, but first they must 'exhaust local remedies'. This could mean that, before applying, they take their case all the way to the Supreme Court and lose, but usually it just means that they must make some effort to resolve their grievance in the UK. If an Act of Parliament or precedent clearly allows the breach of human rights, the European Court of Human Rights may accept that going to a UK court is pointless. Applications must be made within six months. The European Court of Human Rights rejects most complaints, because it does not provide an appeal from national courts. It only wants to hear cases that enable it to clarify the meaning of human rights or to deal with a country that persistently abuses a right. If the victim succeeds, the European Court of Human Rights will grant them 'just satisfaction' – a ruling that the country has breached their human rights. The European Court of Human Rights sometimes awards moderate damages and can order costs. There is an appeal to the Grand Chamber. Judgments are enforced by the Committee of Ministers of the Council of Europe. They will try to persuade the state to cease the breach of human rights. Non-compliance can lead to the country being suspended or expelled from the council, but these powers have never been used. The UK has a good record of compliance. **Practice example 8.4** illustrates the role of the European Court of Human Rights.

Practice example 8.4

Your client has lost his human rights claim in the Court of Appeal and been refused permission to appeal to the Supreme Court. He asks about applying to the European Court of Human Rights. What advice would you give?

The client has exhausted local remedies. The **European Court of Human Rights** would probably refuse to hear the case if they had dealt with similar complaints before. If the court did hear the case and the client was successful, judgment would be given against the UK. These judgments cannot be enforced in a UK court, so the client would have to wait for the UK government to comply.

Summary: convention rights	
WHAT are convention rights?	The articles of the ECHR that are enforceable under the Human Rights Act 1998.
HOW are they used?	Enforced in UK courts and in the European Court of Human Rights.
WHO are they used by?	Victims under UK jurisdiction.

■ KEY POINT CHECKLIST

This chapter has covered the following key knowledge points. You can use these to structure your revision, making sure to recall the key details for each point, as covered in this chapter.

- The Human Rights Act 1998 allows the ECHR to be enforced in UK courts.
- The UK courts must take account of the case law of the European Court of Human Rights.
- The UK courts must try to interpret UK law to be compatible with convention rights.
- The UK courts may declare a law to be incompatible with convention rights.
- Parliament is sovereign and may choose to legislate in a way that is incompatible with convention rights.
- Victims of a violation of human rights may enforce the Act against a public authority.
- Victims may still apply to the European Court of Human Rights.

■ KEY TERMS AND CONCEPTS

- declaration of incompatibility (**page 138**)
- public authority (**page 139**)
- victim (**page 141**)
- proportionality (**page 145**)

■ SQE1-STYLE QUESTIONS

QUESTION 1

The Supreme Court has made a declaration that a section of an Act of Parliament is incompatible with human rights.

Which of the following statements best summarises the legal position?

A. Parliament is obliged to repeal the offending section.

B. Parliament may repeal the offending section.

C. Parliament may refer the matter back to the Supreme Court.

D. Parliament may wait for the result of any appeal to the European Court of Human Rights.

E. Parliament is obliged to compensate the complainant who brought the case.

QUESTION 2

A client alleges that his human rights have been violated and wishes to apply to the European Court of Human Rights.

Which of the following statements best describes how the application should be made?

A. The client's case must be referred to the European Court of Human Rights by the Supreme Court.

B. The client's case may be referred to the European Court of Human Rights by any UK court or tribunal.

C. The client must appeal from the final decision of a UK court.

D. The client may apply to the European Court of Human Rights.

E. The client's case may be referred to the European Court of Human Rights by the High Court or any higher court.

QUESTION 3

Section 2 of the Human Rights Act 1998 states that 'a court or tribunal determining a question which has arisen under this Act in connection with a Convention right must take into account any judgment of the European Court of Human Rights'.

Which of the following statements is the most accurate interpretation of the meaning of these words?

A. A court or tribunal must follow a judgment of the European Court of Human Rights.

B. A court or tribunal may choose to follow a judgment of the European Court of Human Rights.

C. A court or tribunal should normally follow a judgment of the European Court of Human Rights.

D. A court or tribunal must consider a judgment of the European Court of Human Rights.

E. A court or tribunal must not follow a judgment of the European Court of Human Rights.

QUESTION 4

Under the Human Rights Act 1998 it is unlawful for a public authority to act in a way that is incompatible with a convention right. A 'victim' of the unlawful act' may bring proceedings against the authority.

Which of the following best describes the meaning of victim?

A. A claimant who is aggrieved by the unlawful act.

B. A claimant who wishes to stop the unlawful act.

C. A claimant who has suffered physical harm from the unlawful act.

D. A claimant who has suffered financial loss from the unlawful act.

E. A claimant who has been personally affected by the unlawful act.

QUESTION 5

Under the Human Rights Act 1998 claims may be brought against a 'public authority'.

Which of the following statements best defines the meaning of public authority?

A. A public authority is a person (natural or legal) who receives public funding.

B. A public authority is a person (natural or legal) who performs a governmental function.

C. A public authority is a person (natural or legal) who has statutory powers.

D. A public authority is a person (natural or legal) who performs functions of a public nature.

E. A public authority is a person (natural or legal) who performs a public service.

■ ANSWERS TO QUESTIONS

Answers to 'What do you know already?' questions at the start of the chapter

1) False. The rights have existed since 1953, but could not be directly enforced in UK courts until the Human Rights Act came into force in 2000.
2) The correct answer was (a). The courts need only take account of judgments from the European Court of Human Rights.
3) The correct answer was (c). The courts are obliged to interpret Acts of Parliament to be compatible with convention rights and may make a declaration of incompatibility if they cannot. However, Parliament is sovereign, and the courts cannot declare an Act of Parliament void.
4) The correct answer was (a). A victim of an unlawful Act may bring proceedings against a public authority.
5) False. In addition to proceedings in the UK courts, applications to the European Court of Human Rights are still permitted.

Answers to end-of-chapter SQE1-style questions

Question 1:
   The correct answer was B. This is because Parliament is sovereign. The courts cannot tell Parliament what it must do.
Question 2:
   The correct answer was D. This is because the UK is a party to the ECHR and must accept the right of victims to complain to that court. However, there is no route of appeal linking the UK courts to the European Court of Human Rights.
Question 3:
   The correct answer was C. The UK courts have interpreted s 2 to mean that the UK courts should normally follow decisions of the European Court of Human Rights.
Question 4:
   The correct answer was E. This is the definition adopted by the European Court of Human Rights. Section 7(6) of the Human Rights Act 1998 states that UK courts should use the same test.
Question 5:
   The correct answer was D. That is the definition in the Act. The other answers are the factors that a court should consider when deciding whether a person is a public authority.

■ KEY CASES, RULES, STATUTES AND INSTRUMENTS

• The Human Rights Act 1998

The SQE1 Assessment Specification does not require you to remember the names of the following two cases, but the principles that they lay down are important:

• *R (Alconbury Developments Ltd) v Secretary of State for the Environment* [2003] 2 AC 295 – UK courts will usually follow decisions of the European Court of Human Rights.

• *Parishional Church Council of Aston Cantlow v Wallbank* [2003] 3 All ER 1213 – this case describes the main features of a public authority.

9

European Union law

■ MAKE SURE YOU KNOW

This chapter will cover the place of European Union (EU) law in the UK constitution. It will explain parliamentary sovereignty and the EU, the sources of **retained EU law**, the categories/status/interpretation of retained EU law, the modification/withdrawal of retained EU law and parliamentary sovereignty and retained EU law. You will need to know about these topics and be able to apply them to scenarios, problems and situations for your SQE1 assessment.

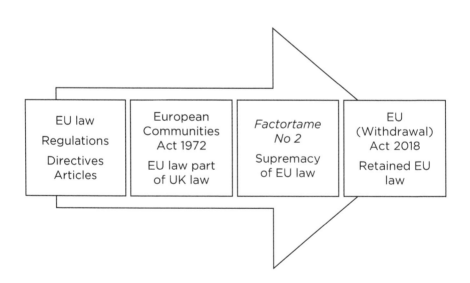

| EU law
Regulations
Directives
Articles | European
Communities
Act 1972
EU law part
of UK law | *Factortame
No 2*
Supremacy
of EU law | EU
(Withdrawal)
Act 2018
Retained EU
law |

■ SQE ASSESSMENT ADVICE

As you work through this chapter, remember to pay particular attention in your revision to:
• the sources of retained EU law – the EU's law-making powers
• EU law and UK law
• withdrawal from the EU.

■ WHAT DO YOU KNOW ALREADY?

Have a go at these questions before reading this chapter. If you find some difficult or cannot remember the answers, make a note to look more closely at that subtopic during your revision.

1) Member states of the EU must obey an EU regulation, but do not have to obey an EU directive. True or false?
   [The different types of EU law, page 155]

2) Why was the European Communities Act (ECA) 1972 constitutionally important?
   a) it altered the doctrine of parliamentary sovereignty
   b) it allowed the UK to join an international organisation
   c) it allowed delegated legislation to amend Acts of Parliament.
   [Sovereignty and EU law, page 157]

3) What did the *Factortame* case decide?
   a) Spanish fishermen could not fish in UK waters
   b) the EU could repeal UK Acts of Parliament
   c) the ECA 1972 gave sovereignty to EU law.
   [Sovereignty and EU law, page 157]

4) After leaving the EU, which of the following statements is the most accurate?
   a) EU law remains in force in the UK
   b) EU law made before 31 January 2020 becomes UK law
   c) EU law made before 31 December 2020 remains in force in the UK.
   [The EU (Withdrawal Act) 2018, page 159]

5) Why did the EU (Withdrawal Agreement) Act 2020 need to be passed?
   a) to implement the terms of the Withdrawal Agreement into UK law
   b) to notify the EU that the UK had left
   c) to agree the terms of the withdrawal with the EU.
   [The Withdrawal Agreement: Trade and Cooperation Agreement, page 162]

THE SOURCES OF RETAINED EU LAW: THE EU'S LAW-MAKING POWERS

The European Economic Community and the European Atomic Energy Community were created by the Treaty of Rome in 1957. The founder members were France, Germany, Belgium, the Netherlands, Luxemburg and Italy. The UK joined in 1973 and the communities became the EU in 1992. After the UK's withdrawal in 2020, 27 European states remain members of the EU.

Uniquely for an international organisation, the member states agreed that the EU would have the power to legislate for its members. This section will enable you to revise:
• the Court of Justice of the European Union
• the different types of EU law
• the supremacy of EU law.
It is still important to know about EU law for two reasons. First, the EU law that applied in the UK before withdrawal remains in force. It is now known as **retained EU law**.

Key term: retained EU law

EU law that was in force in the UK before '**exit day**' on 31 January 2020 remains in force. However, it is no longer EU law because it is converted into domestic law by the EU (Withdrawal) Act 2018.

Second, the Withdrawal Agreement between the UK and the EU is directly enforceable in UK courts, and must be interpreted by the UK courts in accordance with EU law.

The Court of Justice of the European Union

The EU created the European Court of Justice (ECJ), now known as the Court of Justice of the European Union (CJEU), to interpret EU law and enforce it throughout the EU. The European Commission can take a member state to the court and member states can take each other to the court. Ordinary citizens cannot apply directly to the CJEU. They must start their case in the court of a member state and await referral to the CJEU. Before leaving the EU, any UK court or tribunal could refer a case to the CJEU for a ruling on the meaning of EU law. If a case involved EU law, the Supreme Court was obliged to make a reference. The EU (Withdrawal) Act 2018 stopped these references from the UK.

The CJEU insists that EU law is obeyed and interpreted in the same way in every member state. To that end the court devised the principle of **direct effect**.

Key term: direct effect

Claimants can enforce rights created by EU law in *national* courts. There is vertical direct effect (where the EU law may only be enforced against state authorities) and horizontal direct effect (where the EU law may also be enforced against private persons and organisations).

The different types of EU law

The different types of EU law take effect in different ways.

Regulations

Regulations are binding and directly applicable in every member state. National legislation is not required to implement a regulation. They have direct effect if the wording is clear, precise and unconditional enough to create a right. The direct effect is both vertical and horizontal.

Decisions

A decision is binding on the member state to which it is addressed. They also have vertical and horizontal direct effect.

Articles

The case of *Van Gend en Loos v Nederlandse Administratie der Belastingen* [1963] ECR 1 held that articles in the EU Treaty may also have direct effect. If they have clear, unconditional and precise wording, the article creates an individual right enforceable in national courts. These rights were enforceable even if they contradicted national law, because member states had limited their sovereign rights by joining the EU. Articles have both vertical direct effect and horizontal direct effect. CJEU decisions have decided which articles have direct effect. At the time of leaving the EU, the UK estimated that there were 48 articles of the Treaty on the Functioning of the European Union (TFEU) with direct effect.

Directives

Directives instruct member states to make legal changes by a specified date, but leave it up to the state on how best to do it within its own legal system. Some states fail to implement directives or do so incorrectly,

so the CJEU developed vertical direct effect to enforce directives. The conditions for vertical direct effect of a directive are:
• the date for the implementation of the directive has passed
• the terms of the directive are clear, precise and unconditional
• the case is being brought against a *public body*, 'an emanation of the state'.

However, directives cannot be enforced against a non-state, private defendant. The CJEU also developed the concept of indirect effect. Even if a directive does not have direct effect, the national court is required to interpret national law to give effect to the directive.

The Francovich principle

In *Francovich v Italian State* [1992] IRLR 84, the CJEU ordered a state to pay damages to the individual(s) that it had injured by its failure to implement a directive. *Francovich* has been extended to serious breaches of other types of EU law, such as regulations and articles, that injure individuals. If a state commits a serious breach of EU law that causes damage to an individual, the state must compensate that individual.

The supremacy of EU law

The CJEU decided that the EU could only function if EU law applied in the same way in every member state. In the landmark case of *Costa v ENEL [1964] ECR 585* the court declared that member states had made partial transfers of sovereignty to the EU and therefore could not make laws incompatible with EU law. EU law had sovereignty over national law and national courts must set aside conflicting national laws.

Summary: the EU's powers to make law	
WHAT are the law-making powers of the EU?	The EU has the power to make laws that apply within member states.
HOW does this work?	Member states accept this when they join the EU.
HOW is this enforced?	The courts of member states are obliged to apply EU law in preference to national law.

EU LAW AND UK LAW

When the UK joined the EU in 1973, it was obliged to accept existing EU law and the right of the EU to make laws for the UK in the future. This was given effect by the European Communities Act (ECA) 1972. In this section you will be able to revise the effects of that Act, namely:

• The EU could legislate for the UK.
• UK law had to be interpreted to be compatible with EU law.
• Sovereignty and EU law.

The EU may legislate for the UK

The main provisions of the ECA 1972 were:

• Section 2(1) of the ECA 1972 made existing EU law part of UK law and permitted the EU to legislate for the UK. There was no need for the UK to pass legislation to implement new EU laws.
• Section 3 instructed the courts to enforce EU law and decide cases 'in accordance with the principles laid down by ... the European Court'.
• Section 2(2) delegated legislation could be used to make EU law, particularly new directives, part of the law of the UK.
• Section 2(4) delegated legislation could repeal or amend existing Acts of Parliament (see **Chapter 5, page 87**).

UK law must be interpreted to be compatible with EU law

Section 2(2) ECA 1972 stated that 'any enactment passed or to be passed ... shall be construed and have effect subject to the foregoing provisions of this section'. This required judges to interpret UK Acts of Parliament so that they did not conflict with EU law. The courts accepted the direct effect of regulations, articles and directives and learnt to interpret UK legislation so that it conformed to EU law.

Sovereignty and EU law

As we saw in **Chapter 2, page 29**, in the UK constitution, Parliament is regarded as the supreme, sovereign authority. Only Parliament may legislate for the UK, but the EU also claimed this right. These conflicting claims were resolved in *R v Secretary of State for Transport, ex parte Factortame (No 2)* [1991] AC 603. The UK courts could not interpret UK legislation so that it was compatible with EU law, because the UK law explicitly contradicted directly effective articles of the TFEU. The House of Lords stated the position:

• The ECA 1972 voluntarily gave permission to the EU to legislate for the UK.

- The Act also made clear that EU law had sovereignty over UK Acts of Parliament.
- A UK court must 'override any rule of national law found to be in conflict with any directly enforceable rule of community law'.

The ECA 1972 was repealed by the EU (Withdrawal) Act 2018 and permission for the EU to legislate for the UK has been withdrawn.

Exam warning

You are probably aware that the ECA 1972 has been repealed with the UK leaving the EU, but you still need to know about EU law. EU law that applied to the UK at exit has been converted into retained EU law and under the Withdrawal Agreement with the EU, some EU law will still be enforceable in the UK.

Summary: EU law and UK law

WHY did EU law apply in the UK?	The ECA 1972 gave effect to EU law within the UK.
HOW did this work?	UK courts interpreted UK law to conform to EU law. If this was not possible UK courts allowed EU law to override UK law.
WHY has this changed?	Because the ECA 1972 has been repealed.

WITHDRAWAL FROM THE EU

Parliament passed the EU Referendum Act 2015 to authorise the holding of a national referendum on whether the UK should remain a member of the EU. The answer in 2016 was No. This section will enable you to revise:

- the withdrawal process
- the EU (Withdrawal) Act 2018
- the Withdrawal Agreement – Trade and Cooperation Agreement.

The withdrawal process

Article 50 of the Treaty of the European Union (TEU) requires a member state to give notice of withdrawal to the EU 'in accordance with its own constitutional requirements'. The government considered that joining and leaving treaties was a matter of the royal prerogative and wished to notify the EU. The Supreme Court ruled in *R (Miller) v Secretary of State for Exiting the EU* [2017] UKSC 5 that, as leaving the EU would change UK domestic law by altering the constitutional position of the country and changing the rights of residents, an Act of Parliament was required (see **Chapter 4, page 67**). The EU (Notification of Withdrawal) Act 2017 authorised notification and the UK left the EU on 'exit day' 31 January 2020. However, a one-year 'implementation period' was agreed with the EU, and EU law still had effect in the UK until '**implementation period (IP) completion day**' 31 December 2020.

Key term: exit day

Exit day, 31 January 2020, was the day when the UK ceased to be a member of the EU.

Key term: IP completion day

IP completion day, 31 December 2020, was the day when EU law ceased to have effect in the UK.

Revision tip

Try to remember the difference between *exit day*, 31 January 2020 and *IP completion day*, 31 December 2020. It could be useful for the SQE1.

The EU (Withdrawal Act) 2018

Many EU laws applied to the UK, but to repeal them all would be a massive task and leave a large gap in the legal system. Many UK laws were enacted to comply with EU requirements and make little sense if the EU law is removed. The EU (Withdrawal) Act 2018 attempts to provide the solution, by keeping existing EU law and turning it into UK law, known as retained EU law.

The EU may no longer legislate for the UK

Under s 1 of the EU (Withdrawal) Act 2018, the ECA 1972 was repealed on exit day, but continued to have effect until IP completion day. By repealing the ECA 1972, Parliament has withdrawn its permission for the EU to make laws for the UK. No new laws from the EU will be accepted.

Revision tip

It is important to try to remember and understand the terms of the EU (Withdrawal) Act 2018. The section numbers are there for reference, you do not need to remember them for SQE1.

Existing EU law remains in force

Under s 2 of the EU (Withdrawal) Act 2018, 'EU-derived domestic legislation' remains in force. This means that all the delegated legislation made to implement EU law under s 2(2) of the ECA 1972 remains in force. The same applies to any other UK legislation enacted to implement EU law.

Under s 3 of the EU (Withdrawal) Act 2018, 'direct EU legislation', meaning EU regulations, EU decisions directed at the UK and EU tertiary legislation (explanations of EU legislation), which were in force immediately before exit day, become part of domestic law, known as retained EU law.

Section 4 of the EU (Withdrawal) Act 2018 states that any rights, powers, liabilities, obligations, restrictions, remedies and procedures that were available in UK law under the ECA 1972, before exit day, are also retained EU law. This covers articles and directives that have been held by the courts to be directly effective before exit day. However, it is made clear that the right to damages, under the *Francovich* principle, ceased to apply on or after IP completion day.

The supremacy of EU law ends

Section 5 of the EU (Withdrawal) Act 2018 states that the principle of the supremacy of EU law does not apply to any enactment passed after exit day. But, as *existing* EU law is retained, the principle of the supremacy of EU law can continue to apply, where *retained EU law* is not compatible with domestic law made before exit day. If retained EU law conflicts with UK law, made before exit day, the retained EU law must be applied in preference to the UK law.

Look at **Practice example 9.1** for an example of how retained EU law works.

Practice example 9.1

Your client has an equal pay claim and believes that an EU directive grants her greater rights than UK legislation. How would you advise her?

The EU directive only applies in the UK and becomes retained EU law if the CJEU decided that it had direct effect *before* exit day. Then it would have supremacy over the UK legislation if that legislation was also enacted *before* exit day. You also need to warn your client that directives only have vertical direct effect and so can only be enforced against a state employer, not a private employer.

Court interpretation of retained EU Law

Section 6 of the EU (Withdrawal) Act 2018 states that a UK court or tribunal cannot refer cases to the CJEU on or after IP completion day. Nor are they bound by decisions made by the CJEU on or after IP completion day. Courts will have to decide the meaning of retained EU law and must do this in accordance with any retained case law and retained general principles of EU law. They may also consider decisions of the CJEU made *after* IP completion day to help them decide.

The Supreme Court is *not* bound by any retained EU case law and may depart from it, using the same test as for domestic law. This is the 1966 Practice Statement, which states that the House of Lords (now Supreme Court) will normally be bound by its own previous decisions, but may depart from its own previous decision when it appears right to do so. The Court of Appeal is also *not* bound by any retained EU case law and may also depart from the previous decision when it appears right to do so. Lower courts and tribunals are bound by retained EU case law.

Figure 9.1 helps you to quickly revise retained EU law. 'Existing' means existing on exit day on 31 January 2020.

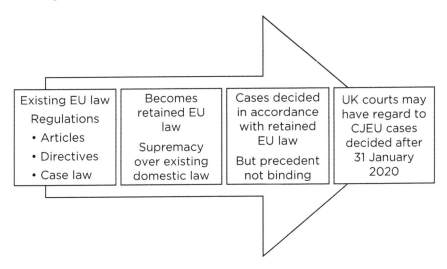

| Existing EU law Regulations • Articles • Directives • Case law | Becomes retained EU law Supremacy over existing domestic law | Cases decided in accordance with retained EU law But precedent not binding | UK courts may have regard to CJEU cases decided after 31 January 2020 |

Figure 9.1: The interpretation of retained EU law

Delegated (secondary legislation)

The EU (Withdrawal) Act 2018 grants extensive power (for two years after the end of the implementation period) to ministers to make delegated legislation to deal with any problems caused by retained EU law. This secondary legislation may amend or repeal Acts of Parliament (see **Chapter 5, page 87**).

The devolved legislatures of Scotland, Wales and Northern Ireland also have these powers, but only upon areas within their devolved competence. It is clear from the Act that the UK Parliament can override the wishes of the devolved legislatures and legislate on these same areas if it wishes (see **Chapter 3, page 54**). The UK Internal Markets Act 2020 grants similar powers to UK government ministers to prevent the devolved institutions replacing retained EU law with laws inconsistent with the wishes of the UK government.

The Withdrawal Agreement: Trade and Cooperation Agreement

The UK finalised its Withdrawal Agreement with the EU in late 2020. The Trade and Co-operation Agreement (TCA), has, as its name suggests, many provisions about trade but also protects the rights of EU citizens resident in the UK, and UK citizens resident in the EU. The Northern Ireland Protocol is also part of the TCA and aims to keep the border between the Republic of Ireland and Northern Ireland open.

The Withdrawal Agreement is enforceable in UK law

Under Article 4, the UK agreed to use EU law to decide the meaning of the Withdrawal Agreement and apply it in preference to UK law. Incompatible UK laws must be disapplied. The agreement can be enforced in UK courts, and rights granted in the agreement can have direct effect in UK courts. CJEU cases decided *before* the end of the transition period must be followed, and the UK courts must have regard to CJEU cases decided *after* the end of that period.

UK law must be interpreted to be compatible with the Withdrawal Agreement

The EU (Withdrawal Agreement) Act 2020 gives the TCA legal effect in UK law and adds s 7A to the EU (Withdrawal) Act 2018. This gives existing rights under the TCA and rights that may be created in future, legal effect in the UK and allows them to be enforced in UK courts. Every enactment past and future is to be read and given effect subject to this requirement. This section has similar effects to the ECA 1972. UK enactments should be interpreted if possible so that they are compatible with the TCA and EU law arising from it. If that is not possible, the TCA and EU law arising from it would have sovereignty over UK Acts of Parliament. Because there is no longer any reference to the CJEU, these questions will have to be decided by UK courts. Section 38 of the EU (Withdrawal Agreement) Act 2020 reaffirms that 'the Parliament of the UK is sovereign' and 'nothing in this Act derogates from' this. This means that the UK Parliament is allowing the EU to legislate for the UK for the limited purposes of the TCA, but can, if it wishes, withdraw that permission with a later Act of Parliament.

Exam warning

There is still uncertainty with regard to how the TCA will be interpreted, and to be sure we must wait for the first cases, when UK courts decide which articles of the TCA have direct effect and whether, if they conflict with UK law, they override Acts of Parliament.

The EU (Future Relationship) Act 2020 also has a general provision in s 29 that existing UK law, including enactments, is to be interpreted as modified by the TCA. You can see how this works in **Practice example 9.2**.

Practice example 9.2

A client has made a contract to ship goods to France. He is concerned because a UK Act of Parliament seems to be contradicted by an article in the TCA. What advice would you give your client?

The EU (Withdrawal Agreement) Act 2020 and EU (Future Relationship) Act 2020 require that, if possible, the UK Act must be interpreted to be compatible with the TCA. If that is not possible, the issue of parliamentary sovereignty arises. The (Withdrawal Agreement) Act suggests that the article of the TCA would have supremacy, unless the UK Act has been passed after 2020 and is expressly worded to contradict the TCA.

Summary: withdrawal from the EU

WHAT is withdrawal from the EU?	The UK has left the EU and is no longer a member state.
HOW is this implemented in UK law?	The EU (Withdrawal) Act 2018 repeals the ECA 1972.
WHAT are the consequences of this?	The EU may no longer legislate for the UK, but existing EU law is converted into retained EU law.

■ KEY POINT CHECKLIST

This chapter has covered the following key knowledge points. You can use these to structure your revision, making sure to recall the key details for each point, as covered in this chapter.

- The EU legislates for its member states. This legislation has direct effect and supremacy over national law.
- The ECA 1972 allowed the EU to legislate for the UK. EU law had supremacy over UK law.
- The EU (Withdrawal Agreement) Act 2020 repealed the ECA 1972. The EU can no longer legislate for the UK.
- Existing EU law (retained EU law) becomes UK law.
- UK courts are no longer bound to follow EU case law.
- Retained EU law can be modified by delegated legislation.
- The Withdrawal Agreement is enforceable in UK courts.

■ KEY TERMS AND CONCEPTS

- retained EU law (**page 154**)
- direct effect (**page 155**)
- exit day (**page 159**)
- IP completion day (**page 159**)

■ SQE1-STYLE QUESTIONS

QUESTION 1

A client is involved in a legal dispute and wishes to know whether an article of the Trade and Cooperation Agreement between the UK and EU can be enforced in a national court.

Which of the following statements best describes how an article is enforced?

A. Depending upon the wording, the article may be directly applicable.

B. Depending upon the wording, the article has direct effect.

C. Depending upon the wording, the article has horizontal direct effect.

D. Depending upon the wording, the article has vertical direct effect.

E. Depending upon the wording, the article has vertical and horizontal direct effect.

QUESTION 2

A man was unaware that EU law still had any effect in the UK, so you need to explain what 'retained EU law' is.

Which of the following statements most accurately describes EU retained law?

A. EU retained law is the EU law that applied when the UK joined the EU.

B. EU retained law is the EU law that was implemented by delegated legislation.

C. EU retained law is the EU law that applied before leaving the EU.

D. EU retained law is the EU law passed by the European Parliament.

E. EU retained law is the EU law made applicable by the Withdrawal Agreement.

QUESTION 3

Leaving the EU changed the relationship between the CJEU and the UK courts.

Which of the following statements is the most accurate description of the current relationship?

A. A UK court may refer questions of EU law to the CJEU.

B. A UK court must refer questions of EU law to the CJEU.

C. A UK court is bound to follow decisions on EU law of the CJEU.

D. A UK court may have regard to decisions on EU law of the CJEU.

E. A UK court must only consider retained EU case law decided by the CJEU.

QUESTION 4

EU law remains in force in the UK as 'retained EU law'. If retained EU law conflicts with UK law, which source of law must UK courts follow?

Which of the following statements is the most accurate statement of the legal position?

A. UK law has supremacy over retained EU law.

B. Retained EU law has supremacy over UK law.

C. Retained EU law has supremacy over UK law enacted before exit day.

D. Retained EU law has supremacy over UK law enacted before IP completion day.

E. Retained EU law has supremacy over UK case law but not UK statute law.

QUESTION 5

The UK completed its Withdrawal Agreement (the Trade and Cooperation Agreement) with the EU in 2020. The UK accepted that the Withdrawal Agreement could be enforced in UK courts.

Which of the following does the Withdrawal Agreement allow claimants in the UK courts to do?

A. Enforce rights created under the Withdrawal Agreement.

B. Enforce EU regulations created under the Withdrawal Agreement.

C. Enforce EU directives created under the Withdrawal Agreement

D. Enforce decisions made by the CJEU.

E. Enforce EU decisions created under the Withdrawal Agreement.

■ ANSWERS TO QUESTIONS

Answers to 'What do you know already?' questions at the start of the chapter

1) False. Member states had to obey both regulations and directives, but the state had a choice about how it would implement a directive.

2) The correct answer was (a). The ECA 1972 did all of (a), (b) and (c), but (a) is the most important.

3) The correct answer was (c). The ECA 1972 allowed the EU to legislate for the UK and that legislation overrode UK law.

4) The correct answer was (b). The EU can no longer legislate for the UK, but the EU law that existed before withdrawal is converted into UK law.

5) The correct answer was (a). The Withdrawal Agreement required the UK to make some changes to its law and this can only be done by Act of Parliament.

Answers to end-of-chapter SQE1-style questions

Question 1:

The correct answer was E. Although the UK has left the EU, it has agreed that articles of the Trade and Cooperation Agreement can have direct effect, meaning that they are enforceable in a UK court. Articles have both vertical and horizontal direct effect.

Question 2:

The correct answer was C. This is because retained EU law is defined as the EU law that applied in the UK on exit day, 31 January 2020.

Question 3:

The correct answer was D. This is because UK courts may no longer refer questions of EU law to the CJEU and are no longer bound by EU law. However, the UK retained existing EU law and a court might want to consider new interpretations of that law made by the CJEU.

Question 4:

The correct answer was C. Although the supremacy of EU law over UK law has ended, supremacy is preserved for the law that existed *before* the UK exited the EU. This is to avoid any accidental changes to the law if EU law suddenly ceased to apply.

Question 5:

The correct answer was A. This is because the UK agreed in the Withdrawal Agreement to allow provisions of the Agreement that meet the conditions for direct effect under union law to be enforced in UK courts.

■ KEY CASES, RULES, STATUTES AND INSTRUMENTS

The SQE1 Assessment Specification does not require you to remember any specific case names or section numbers, but the following case and Act of Parliament contain important principles:

• *R v Secretary of State for Transport, ex parte Factortame (No 2)* [1991] AC 603 – the House of Lords accepted the supremacy of EU law.

• EU (Withdrawal) Act 2018 – this Act explains how EU law becomes retained EU law and how it is to be interpreted.

Index

Milton Keynes UK
Ingram Content Group UK Ltd.
UKHW021808231023
431193UK00010B/139